BUILDING BLOCKS OF THE HUMAN BODY

THE CIRCULATORY SYSTEM

Written by Joseph Midthun

Illustrated by Samuel Hiti

a Scott Fetzer company
Chicago

World Book, Inc.
180 North LaSalle Street
Suite 900
Chicago, Illinois 60601
USA

For information about other World Book publications, visit our website at **www.worldbook.com** or call **1-800-WORLDBK (967-5325)**.
For information about sales to schools and libraries, call 1-800-975-3250 (United States), or 1-800-837-5365 (Canada).

© 2022 World Book, Inc. All rights reserved. This volume may not be reproduced in whole or in part in any form without prior written permission from the publisher.

WORLD BOOK and the GLOBE DEVICE are registered trademarks or trademarks of World Book, Inc.

Library of Congress Cataloging-in-Publication Data for this volume has been applied for.

Building Blocks of the Human Body
ISBN: 978-0-7166-4571-9 (set, hc.)

The Circulatory System
ISBN: 978-0-7166-4574-0 (hc.)

Also available as:
ISBN: 978-0-7166-4582-5 (e-book)

1st printing March 2022

WORLD BOOK STAFF

Executive Committee
President: Geoff Broderick
Vice President, Editorial: Tom Evans
Vice President, Finance: Donald D. Keller
Vice President, Marketing: Jean Lin
Vice President, International Sales: Eddy Kisman
Vice President, Technology: Jason Dole
Vice President, Customer Success: Jade Lewandowski
Director, Human Resources: Bev Ecker

Editorial
Manager, New Content: Jeff De La Rosa
Associate Manager, New Product: Nicholas Kilzer
Sr. Editor: Shawn Brennan
Proofreader: Nathalie Strassheim

Graphics and Design
Sr. Visual Communications Designer: Melanie Bender
Sr. Web Designer/Digital Media Developer: Matt Carrington
Coordinator, Design Development and Production: Brenda B. Tropinski
Book Design: Samuel Hiti

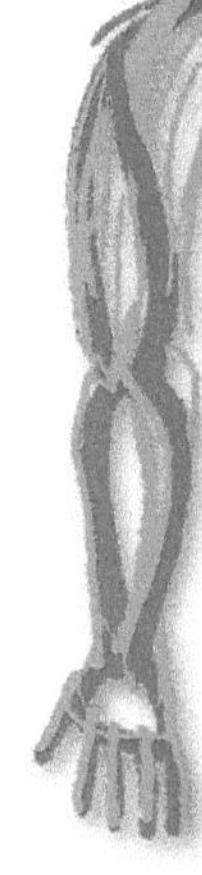

Acknowledgments:
Created by Samuel Hiti and Joseph Midthun
Art by Samuel Hiti
Additional art by David Shephard/The Bright Agency
Additional spot art by Shutterstock
Text by Joseph Midthun

TABLE OF CONTENTS

There is a glossary on page 39. Terms defined in the glossary are in type **that looks like this** on their first appearance.

INTRODUCTION

Your body is made up of millions of tiny living things called **cells.**

Each of these cells needs **oxygen** and **nutrients** from food to keep you alive!

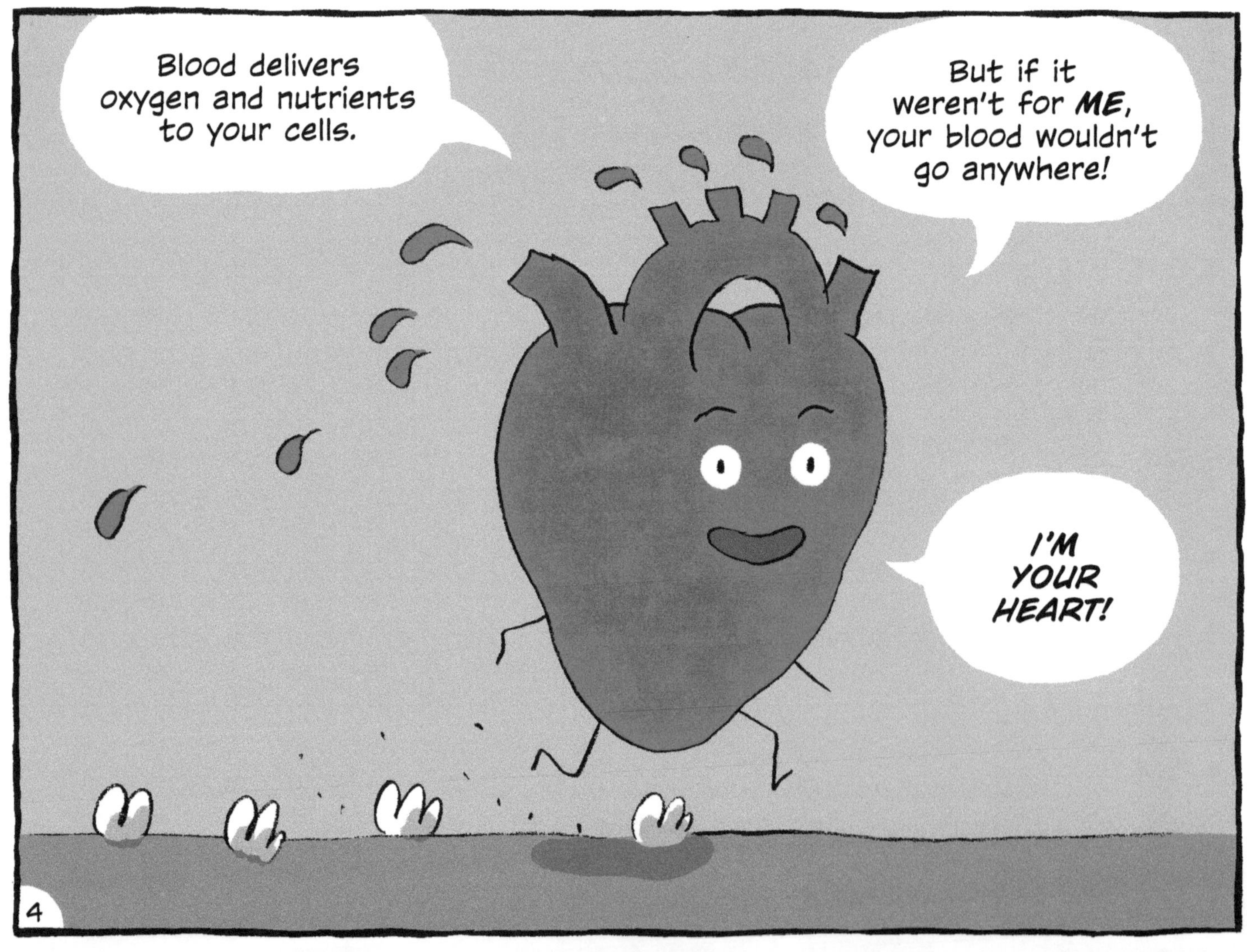

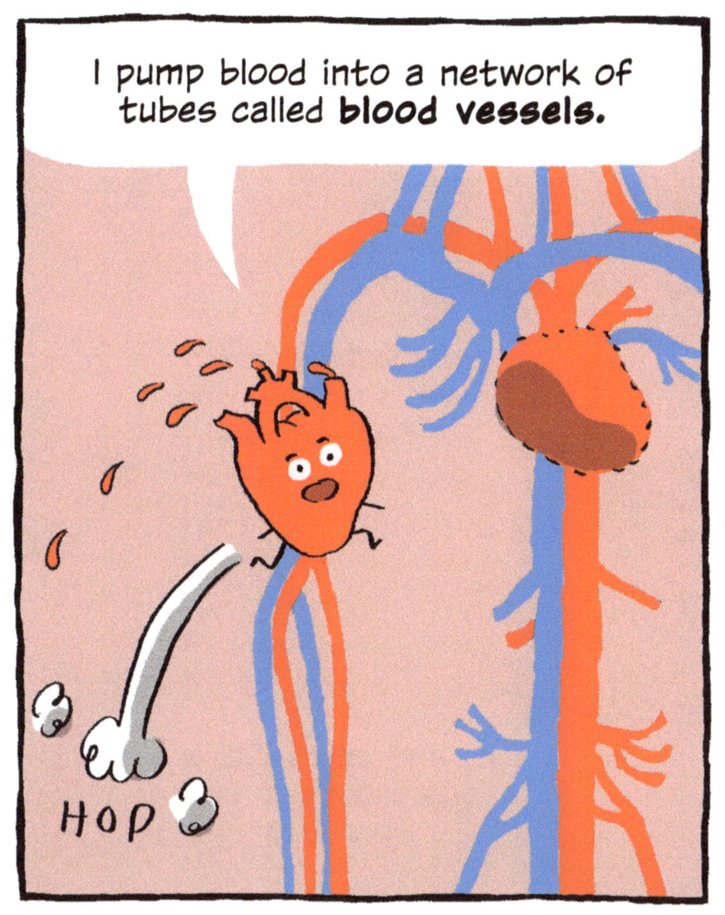

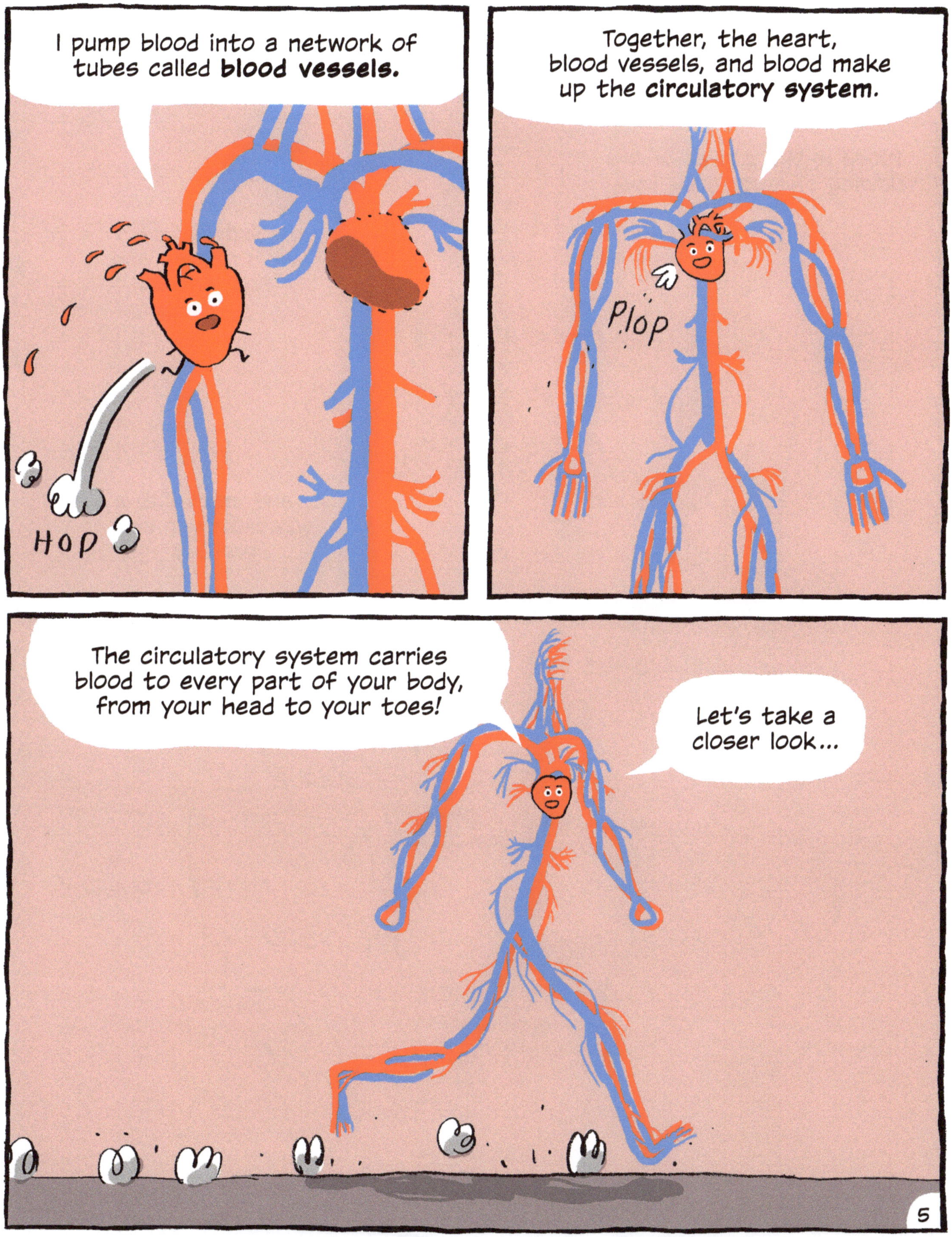

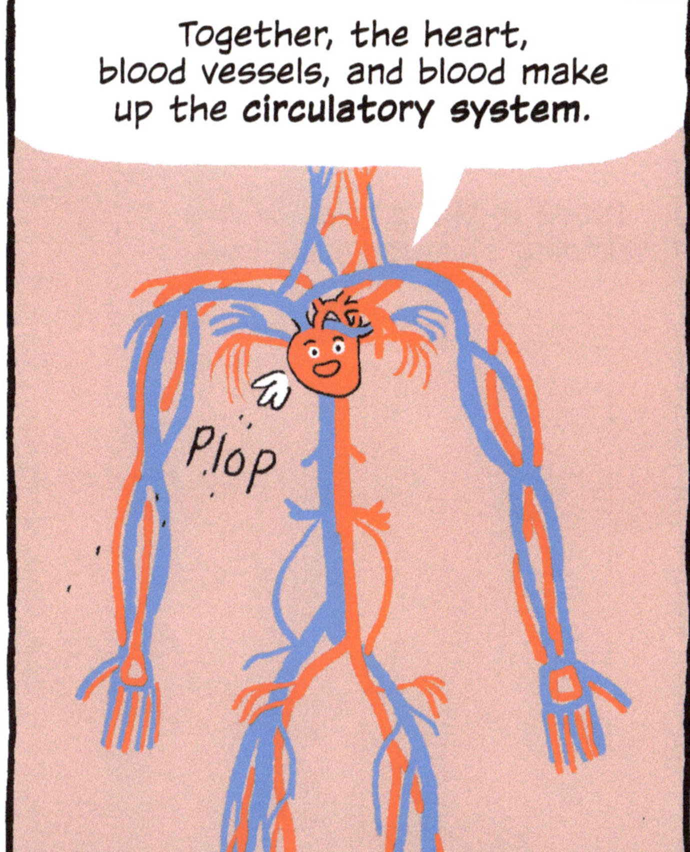

The circulatory system carries blood to every part of your body, from your head to your toes!

Let's take a closer look...

WHAT IS BLOOD?
Blood is like a river of life flowing through your body.
MMM!
SLURP
It supplies cells with oxygen and nutrients...
slurp
...and carries away wastes that cells produce.
THANK YOU!
My pleasure!

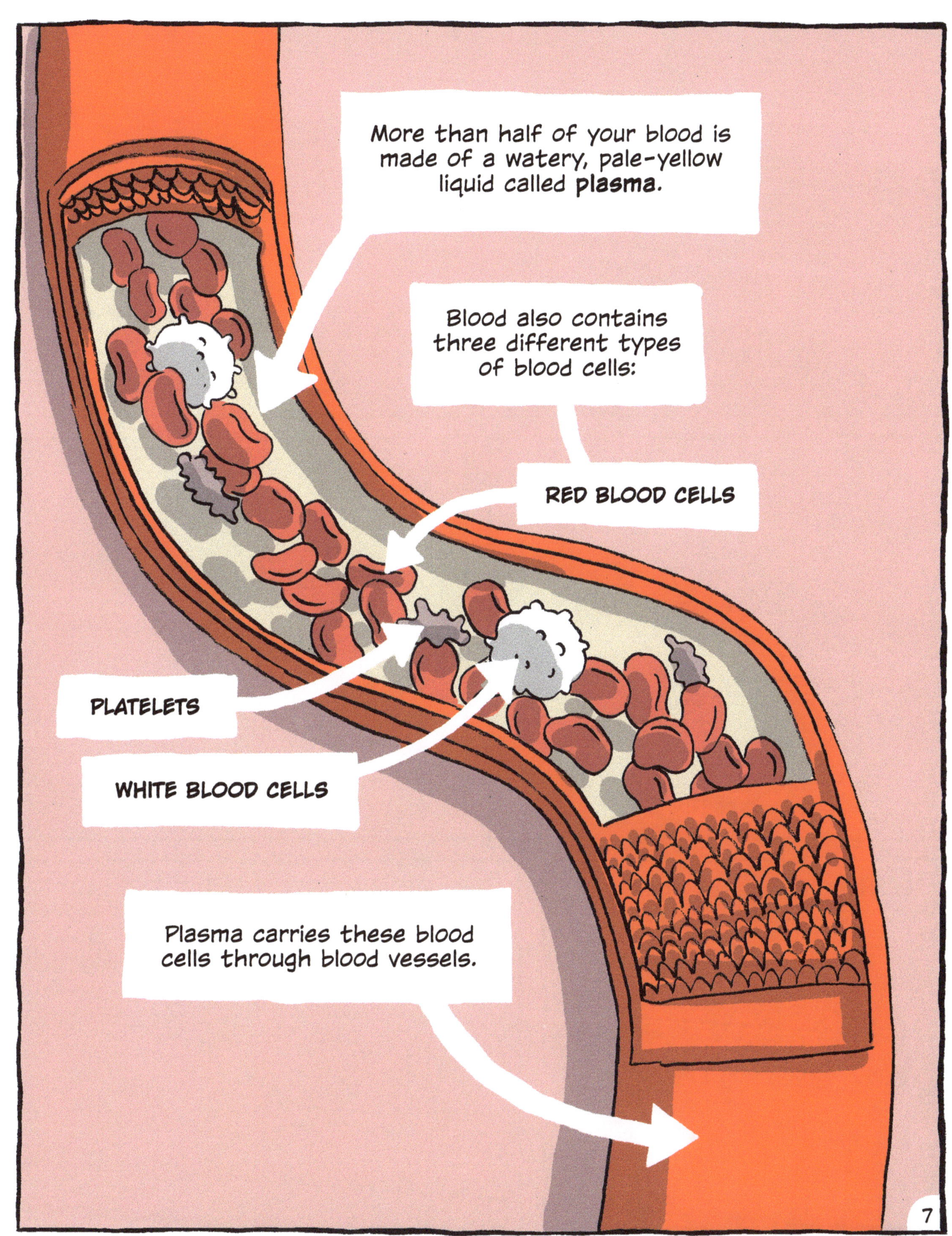
More than half of your blood is made of a watery, pale-yellow liquid called **plasma**.
Blood also contains three different types of blood cells:
RED BLOOD CELLS
PLATELETS
WHITE BLOOD CELLS
Plasma carries these blood cells through blood vessels.

RED BLOOD CELLS
Each type of blood cell has a different job.
Yet, each job is just as important as the other!

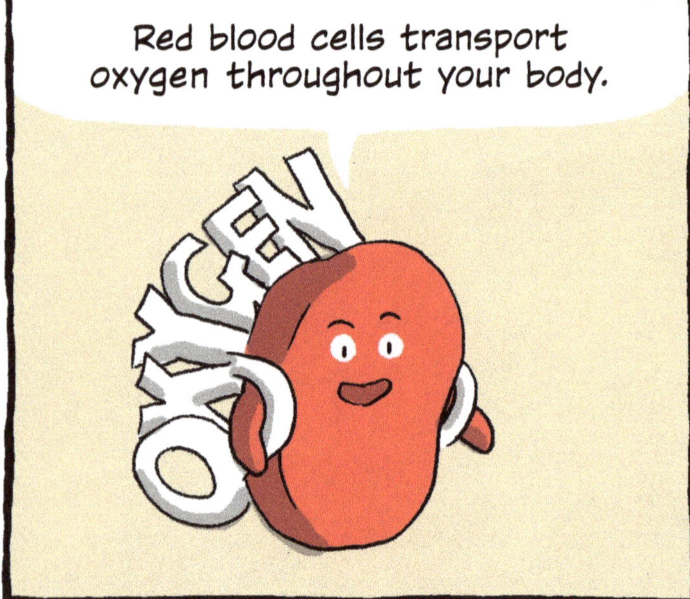
Red blood cells transport oxygen throughout your body.
OXYGEN

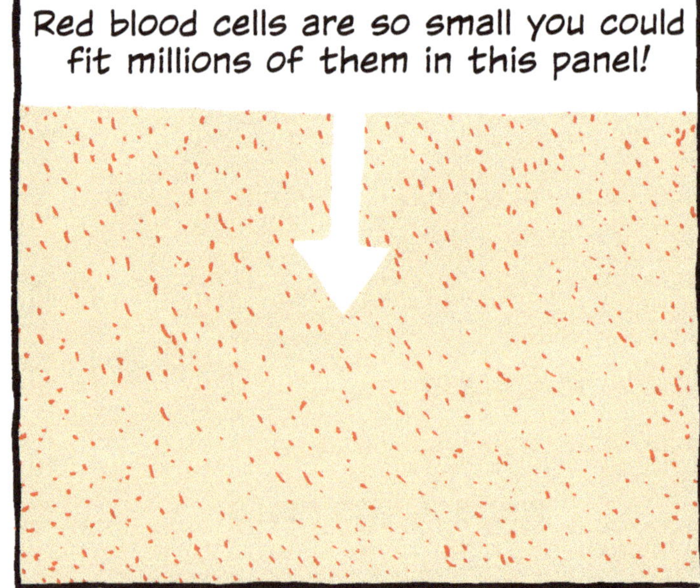
Red blood cells are so small you could fit millions of them in this panel!

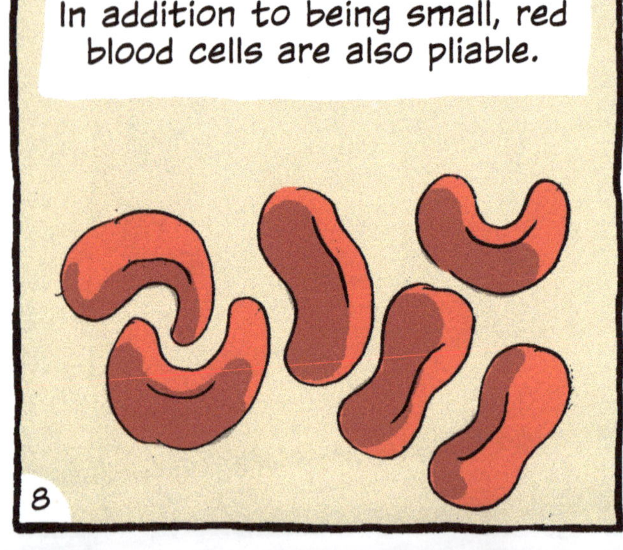
In addition to being small, red blood cells are also pliable.

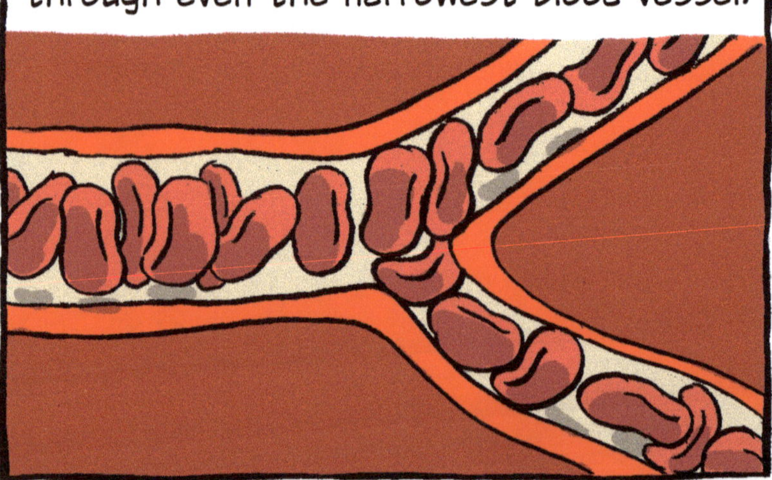
They easily compress and stretch to fit through even the narrowest blood vessel.

oxygen
oxygen
oxygen
oxygen
You might think of red blood cells as oxygen supply trucks and your blood vessels as highways and roads.
oxygen
Right now, there are millions of red blood cells traveling through blood vessels across your entire body!
oxygen
oxygen
oxygen
oxygen
oxygen

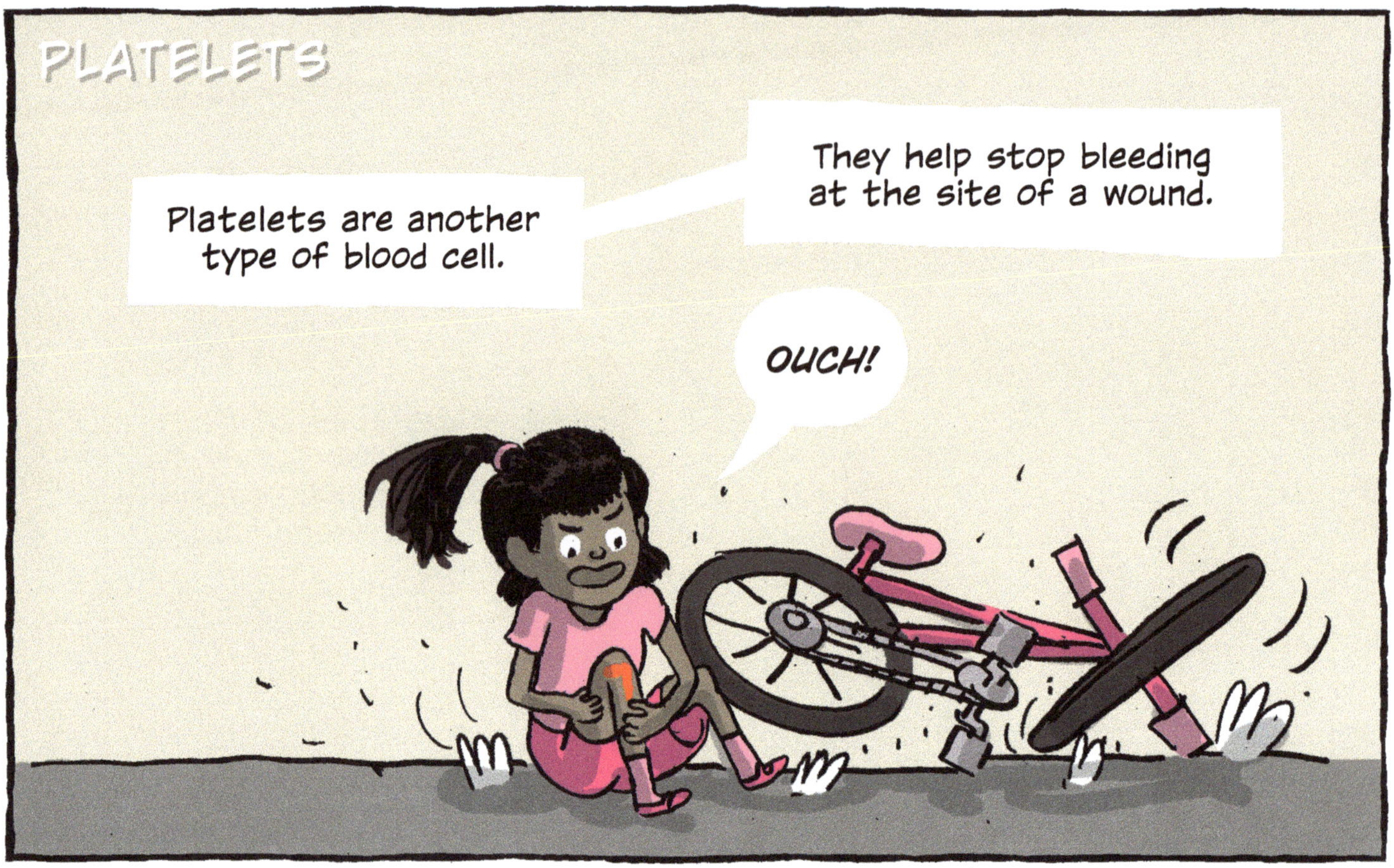

PLATELETS

Platelets are another type of blood cell.

They help stop bleeding at the site of a wound.

OUCH!

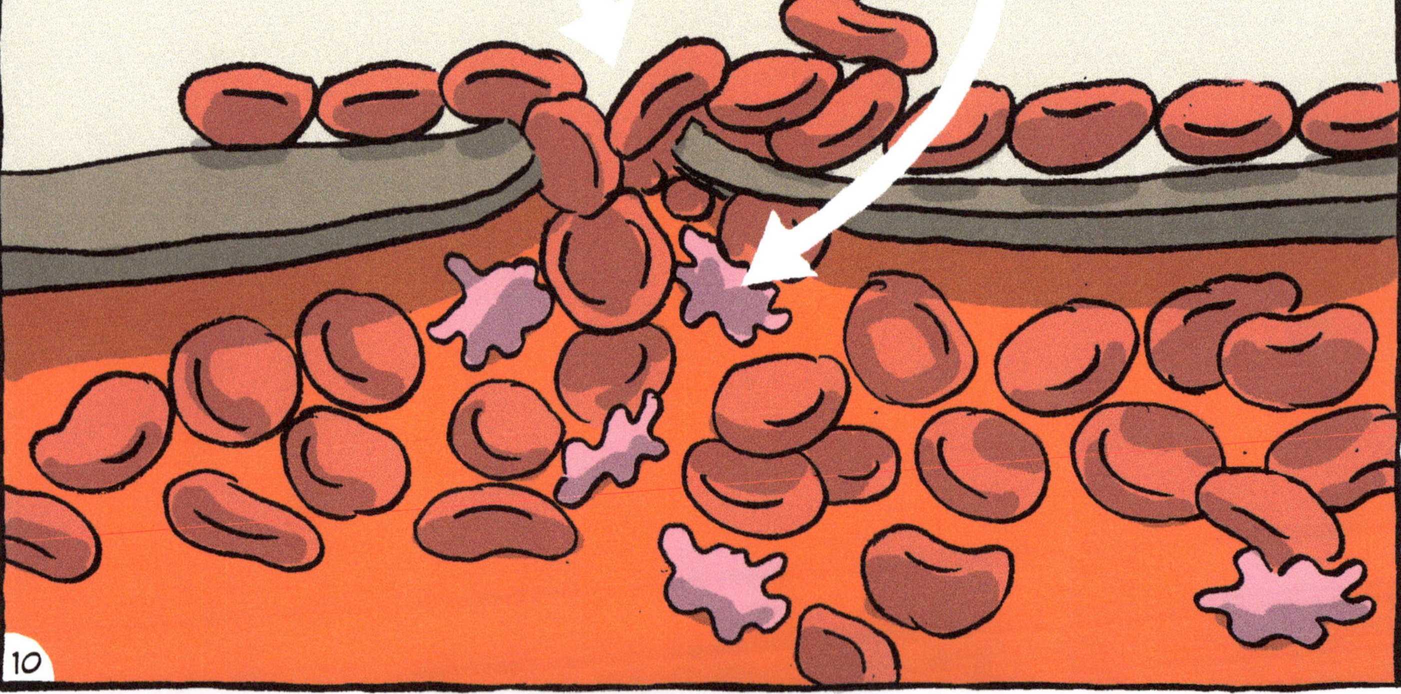

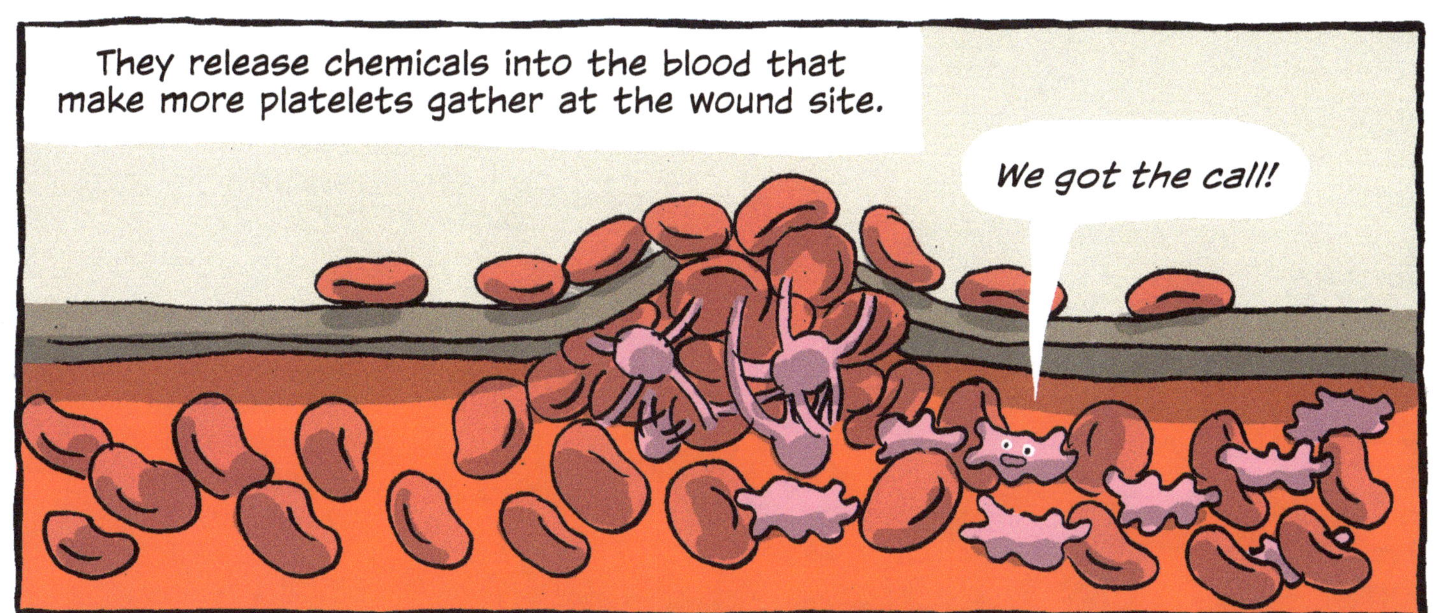
They release chemicals into the blood that make more platelets gather at the wound site.
We got the call!

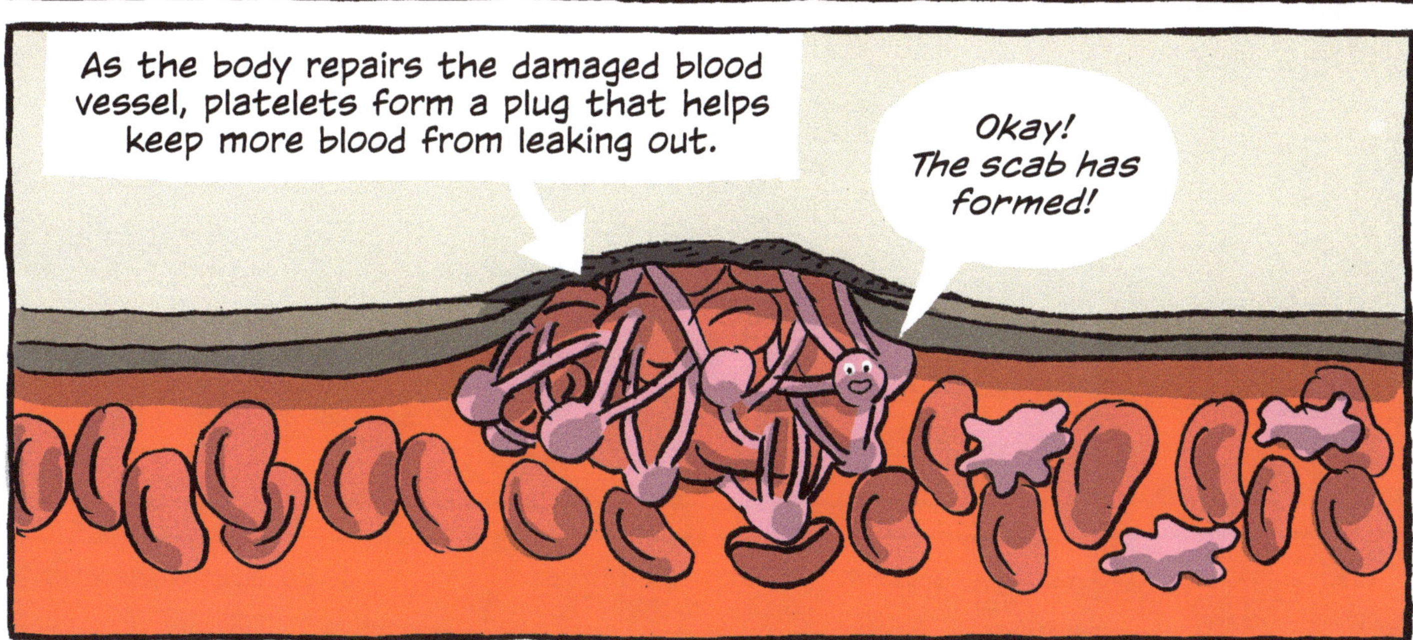
As the body repairs the damaged blood vessel, platelets form a plug that helps keep more blood from leaking out.
Okay! The scab has formed!

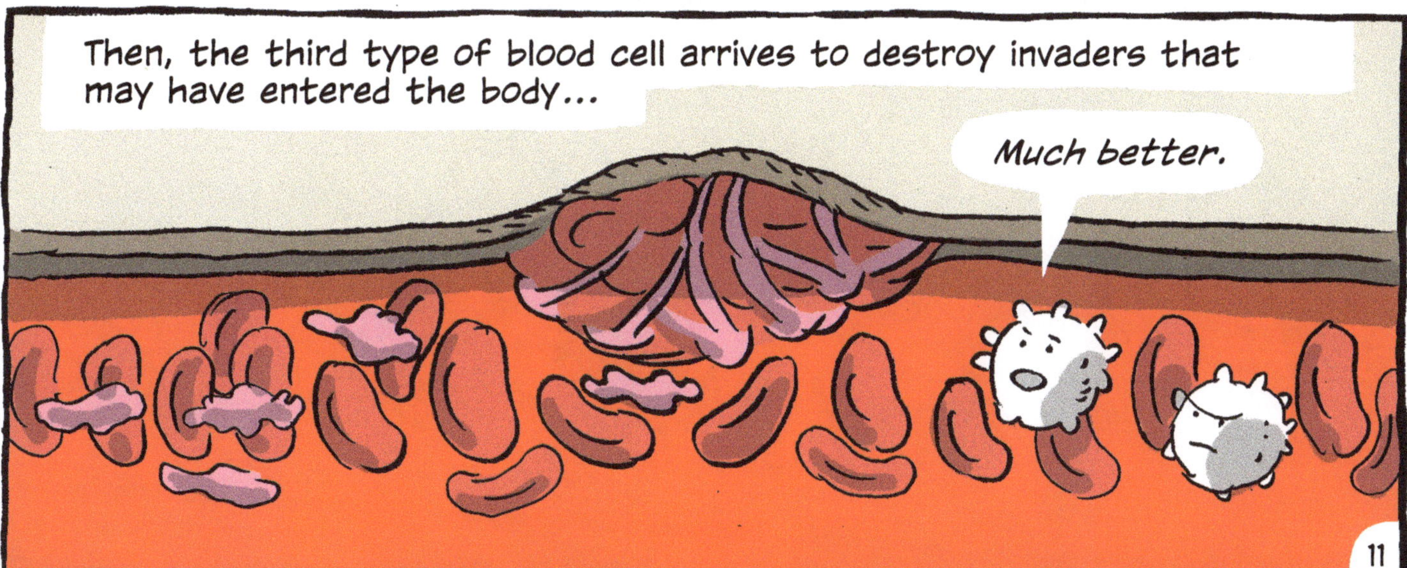
Then, the third type of blood cell arrives to destroy invaders that may have entered the body...
Much better.

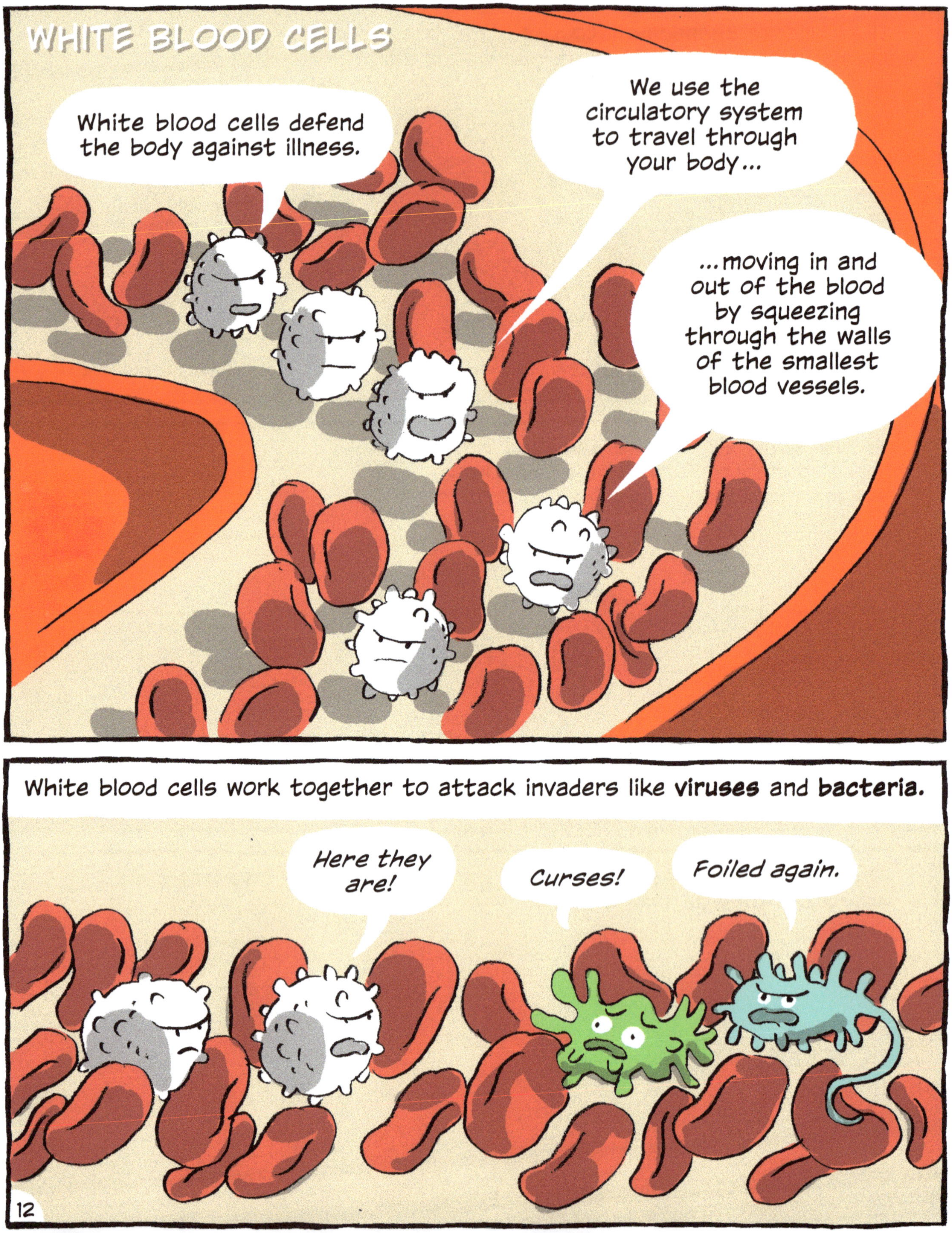

WHITE BLOOD CELLS

White blood cells defend the body against illness.

We use the circulatory system to travel through your body...

...moving in and out of the blood by squeezing through the walls of the smallest blood vessels.

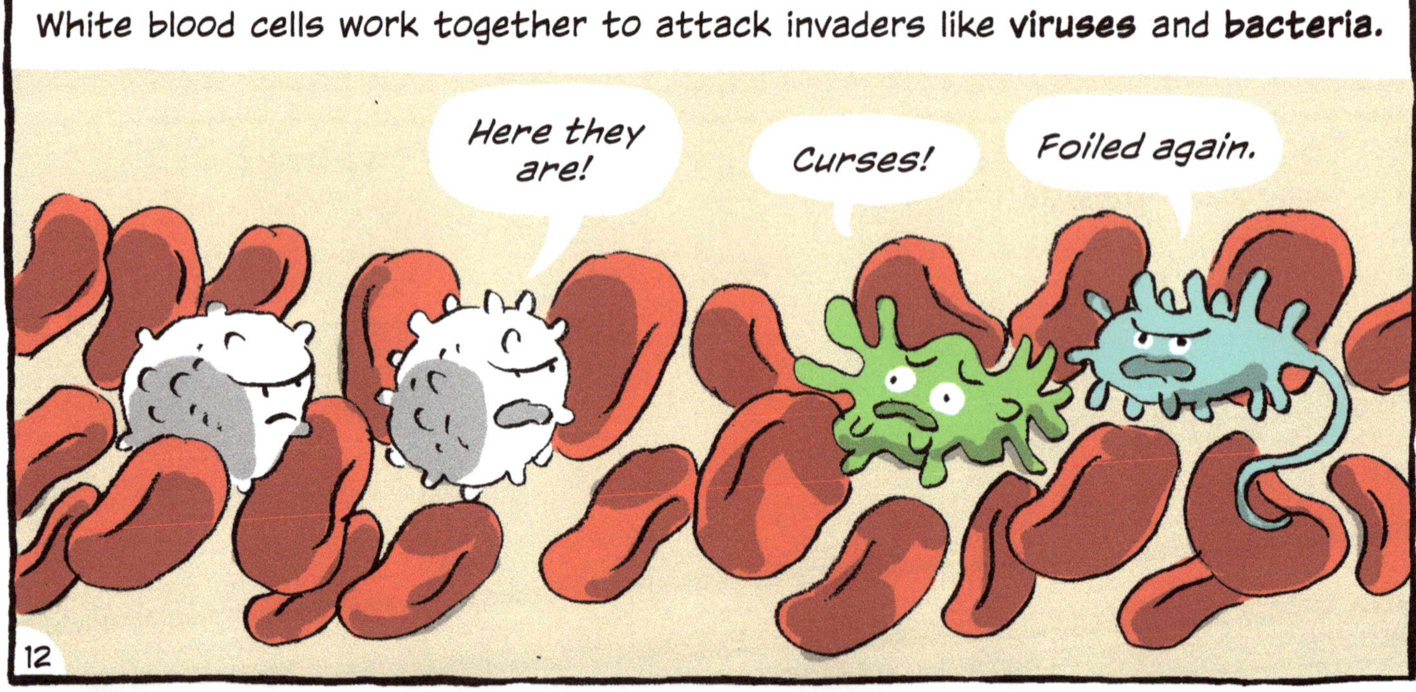

There are five main types of white blood cell, and each has a particular job.

Some release chemicals to fight disease...

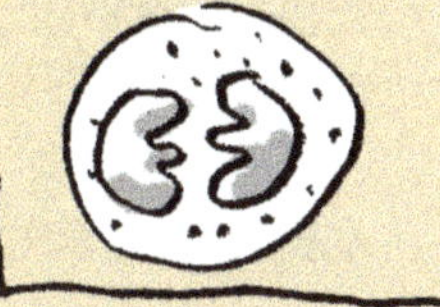

Others swallow up invaders.

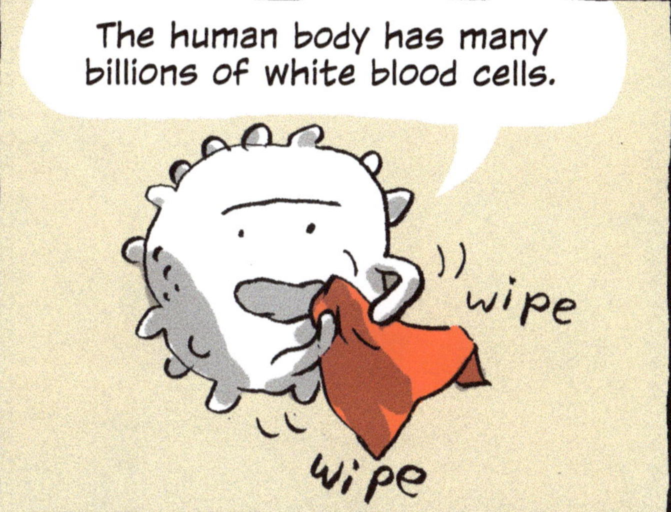

When the body is fighting infection, the number of white blood cells increases.

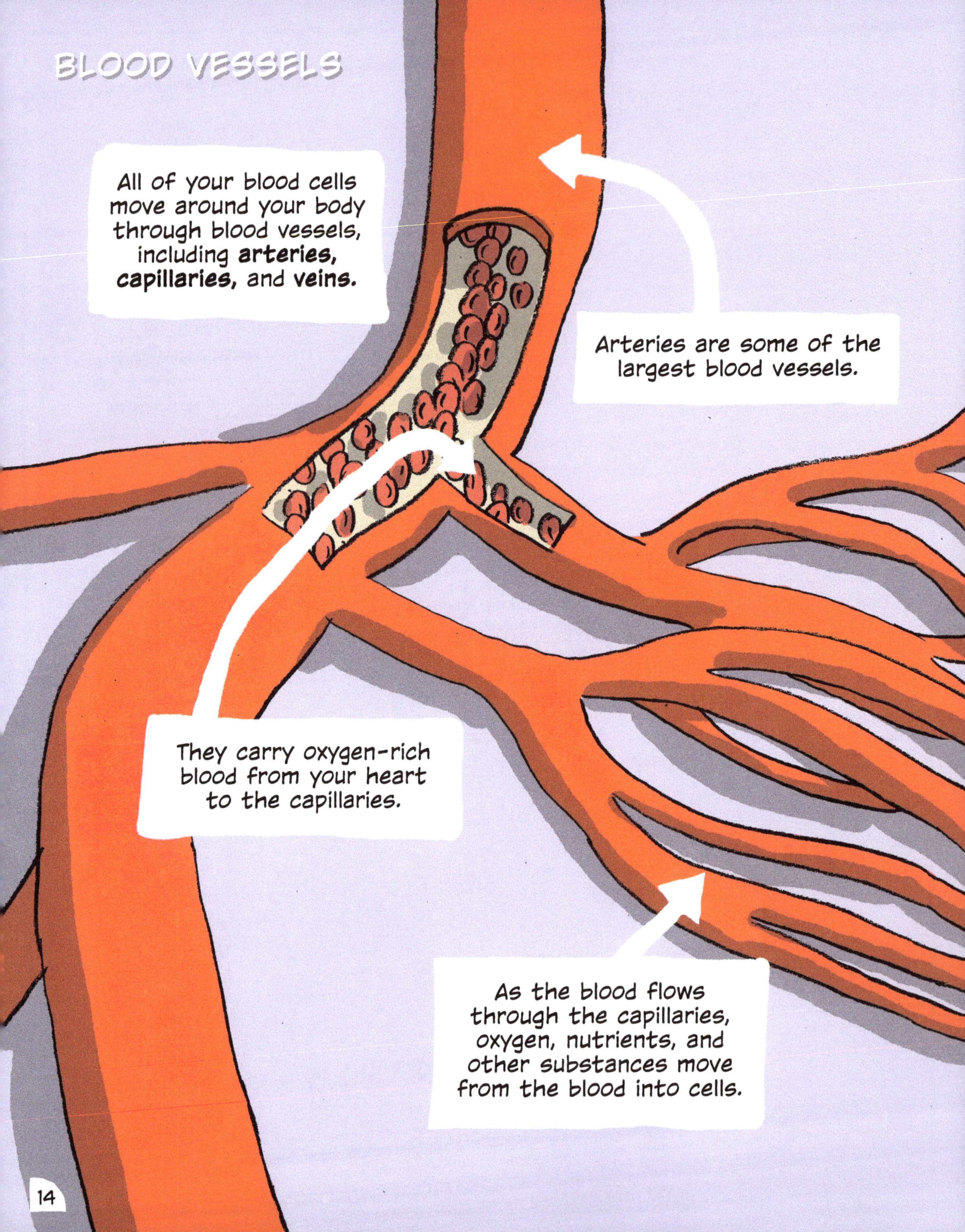
BLOOD VESSELS
All of your blood cells move around your body through blood vessels, including **arteries**, **capillaries**, and **veins**.
Arteries are some of the largest blood vessels.
They carry oxygen-rich blood from your heart to the capillaries.
As the blood flows through the capillaries, oxygen, nutrients, and other substances move from the blood into cells.

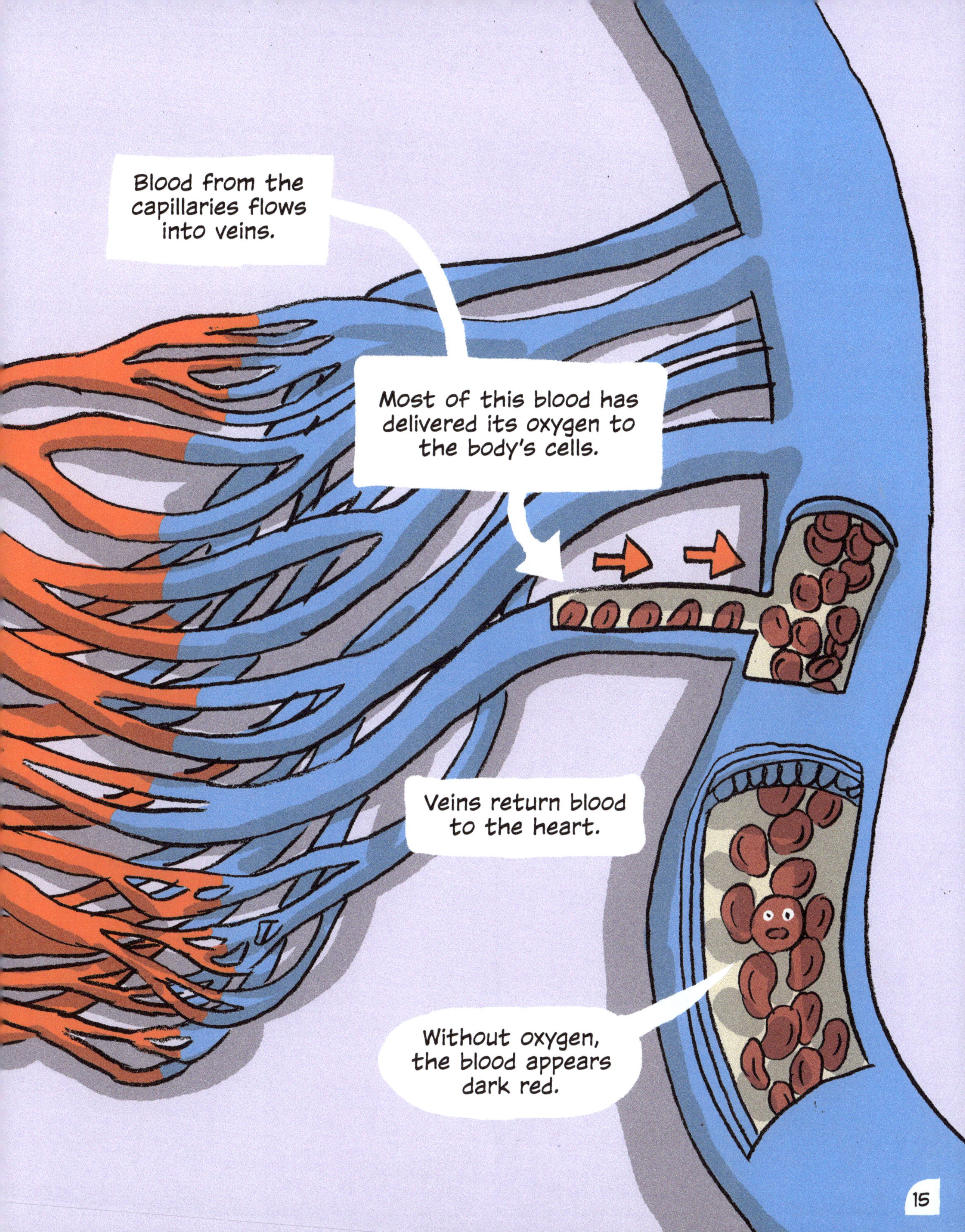
Blood from the capillaries flows into veins.
Most of this blood has delivered its oxygen to the body's cells.
Veins return blood to the heart.
Without oxygen, the blood appears dark red.

THE HUMAN HEART
Your heart works tirelessly to pump blood throughout the body.

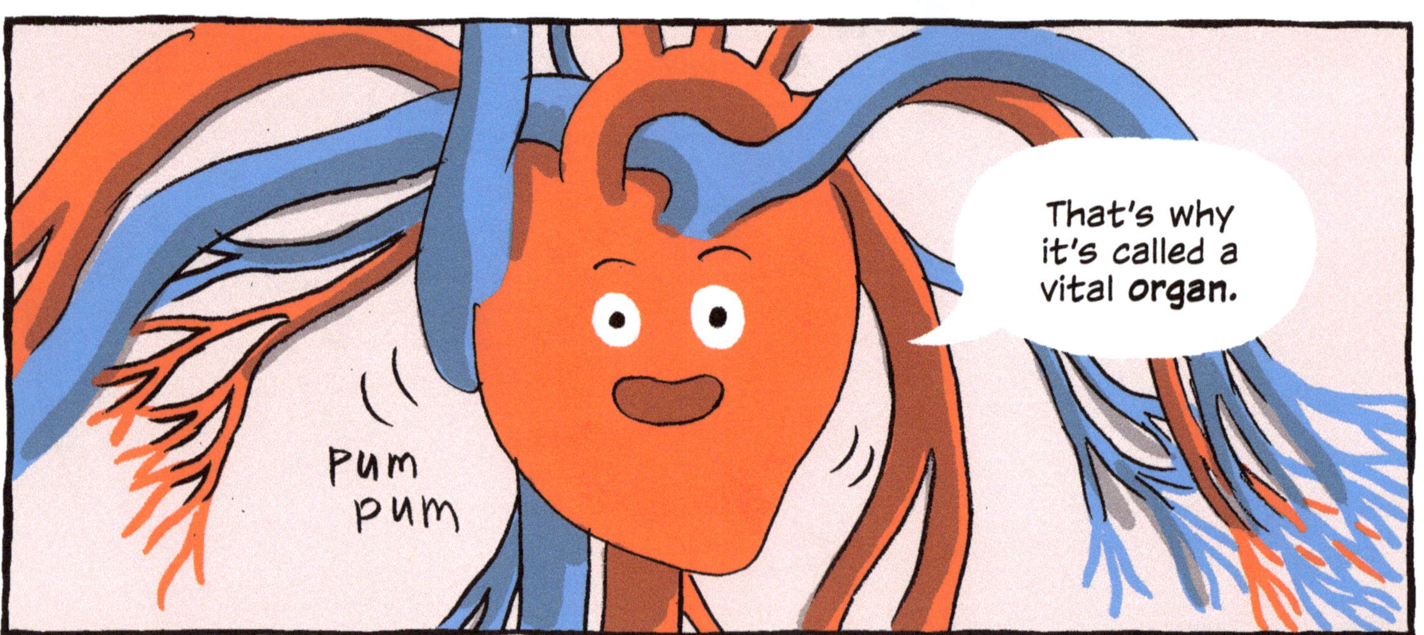
That's why it's called a vital **organ.**
pum pum

Even when you rest...

...or sleep, your heart is still at work!
z.

The heart is made up of muscle **tissue.** This tissue is made of groups of heart muscle cells.

These cells work together to keep the heart beating continuously and rhythmically throughout your life.

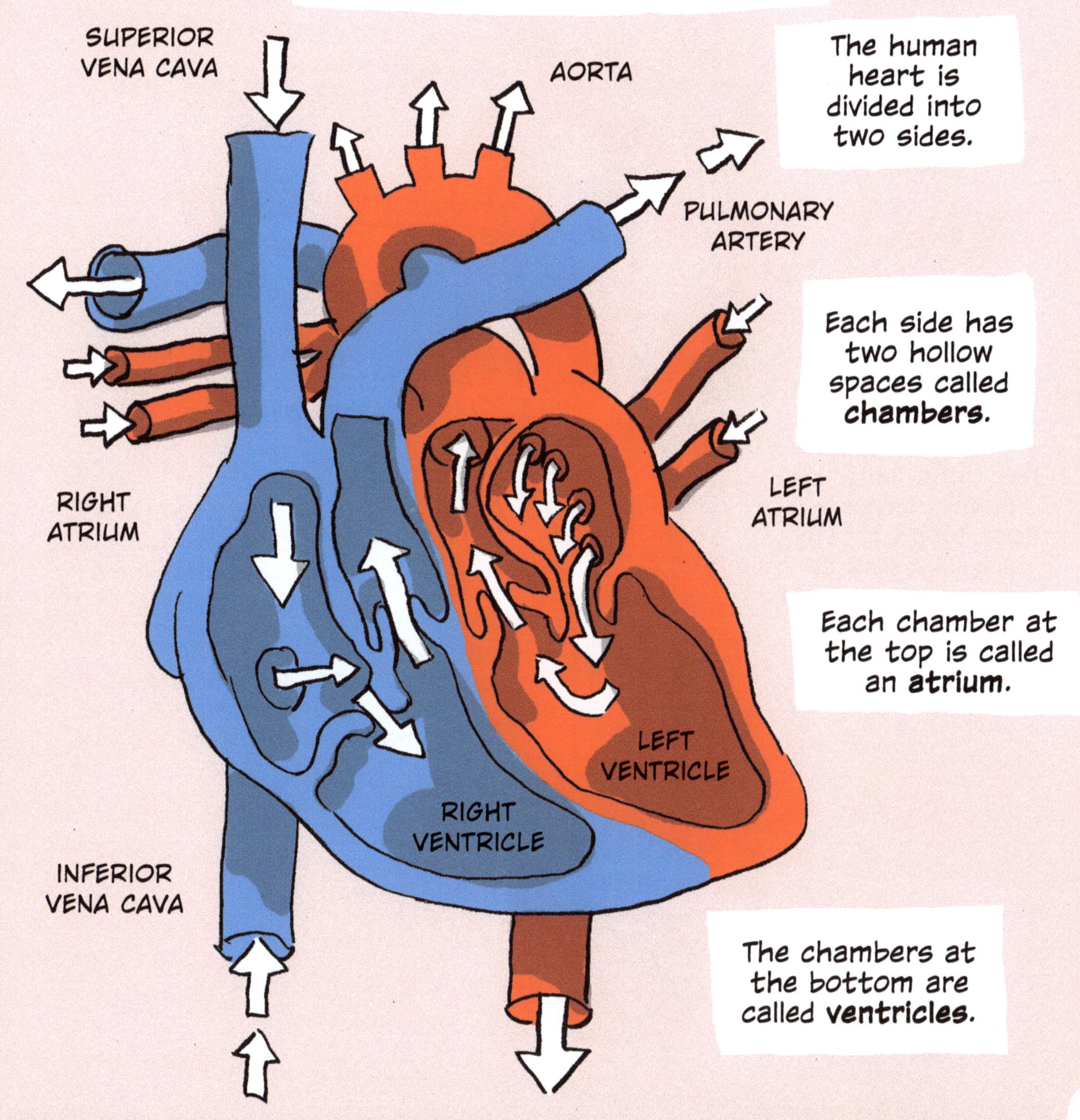

DELIVERING OXYGEN

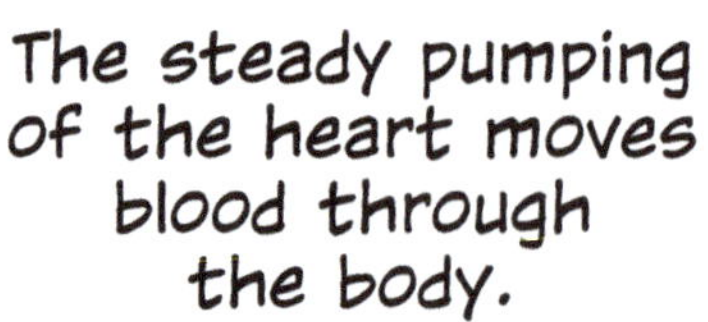

The steady pumping of the heart moves blood through the body.

In fact, the heart is actually ***two*** pumps working at the same time.

Each pump pushes blood through a separate loop of blood vessels.

The right ventricle pumps oxygen-poor blood to the lungs to pick up more oxygen before returning to the heart.

The left ventricle pumps oxygen-rich blood through the body.

This blood leaves the heart through the **aorta,** the main artery of the body.

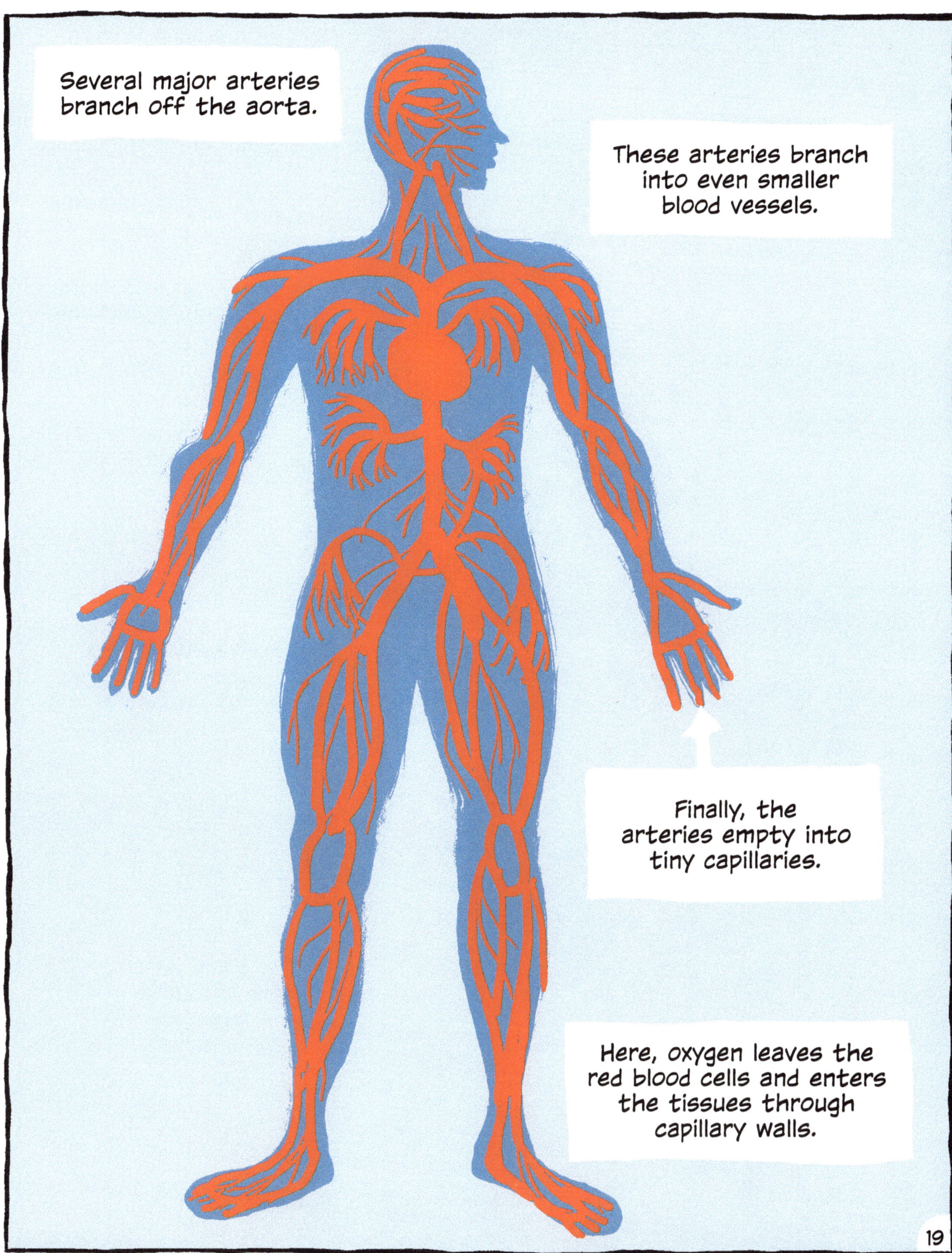
Several major arteries branch off the aorta.
These arteries branch into even smaller blood vessels.
Finally, the arteries empty into tiny capillaries.
Here, oxygen leaves the red blood cells and enters the tissues through capillary walls.

REMOVING WASTES

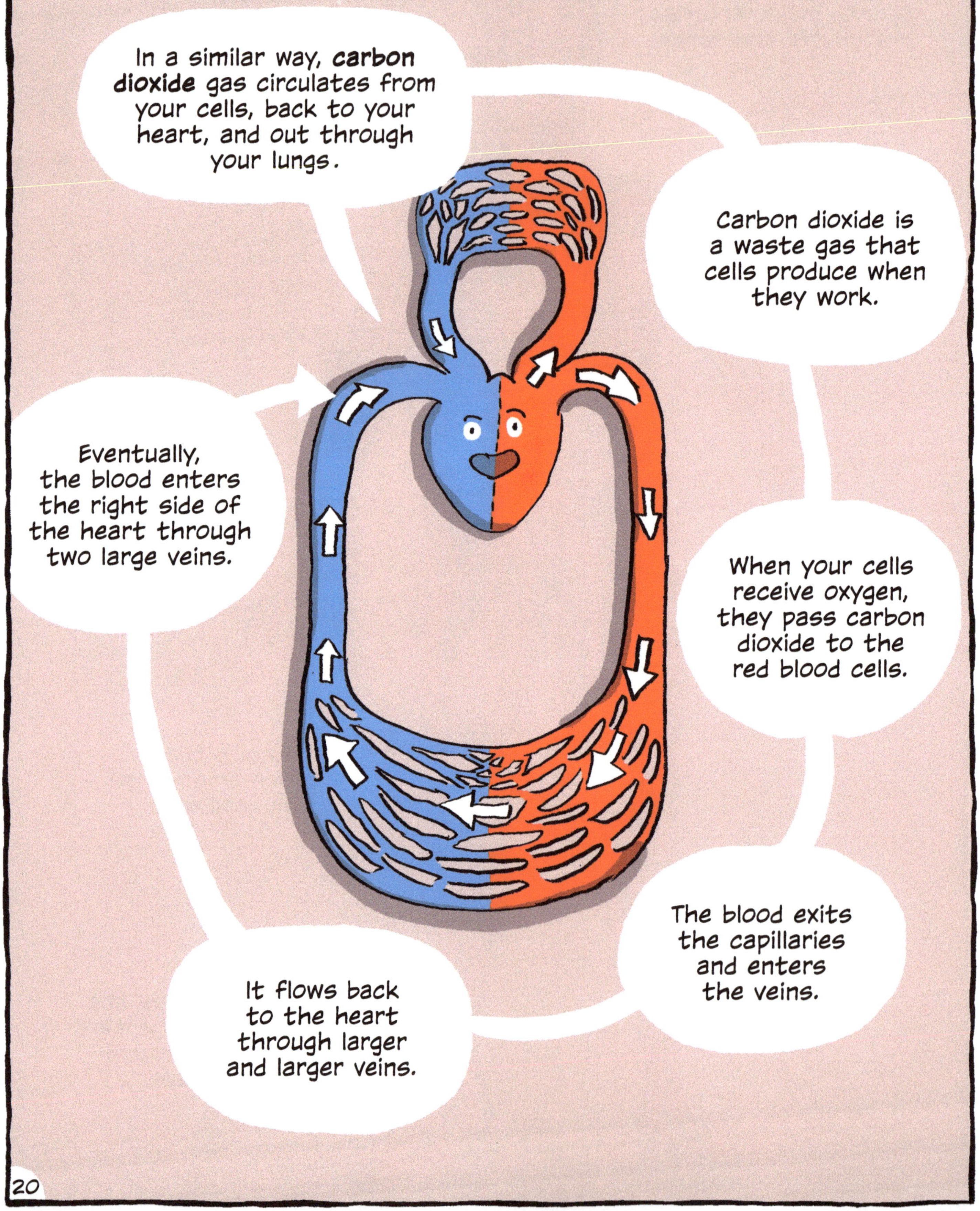

In a similar way, **carbon dioxide** gas circulates from your cells, back to your heart, and out through your lungs.

Carbon dioxide is a waste gas that cells produce when they work.

When your cells receive oxygen, they pass carbon dioxide to the red blood cells.

The blood exits the capillaries and enters the veins.

It flows back to the heart through larger and larger veins.

Eventually, the blood enters the right side of the heart through two large veins.

From the right side of the heart, arteries carry the carbon-dioxide-rich blood to capillaries in the lungs.

Carbon dioxide passes through the capillary walls into the lungs.

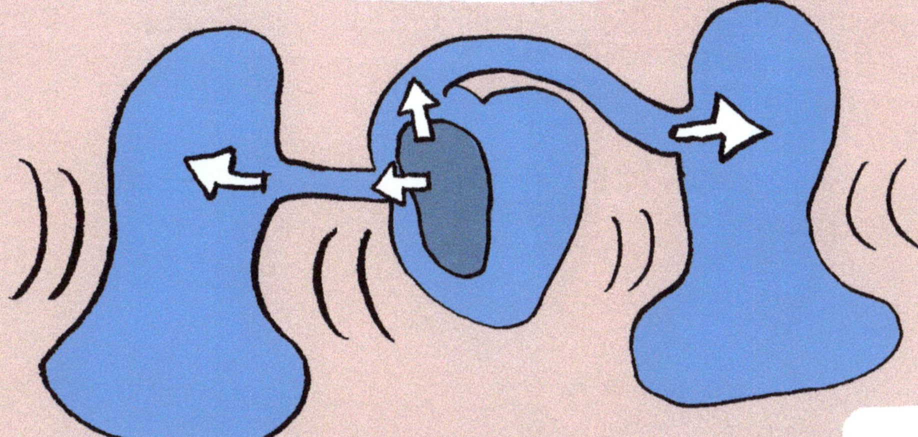

It leaves the body when you exhale.

When you inhale again, oxygen passes from the lungs to red blood cells in a similar way.

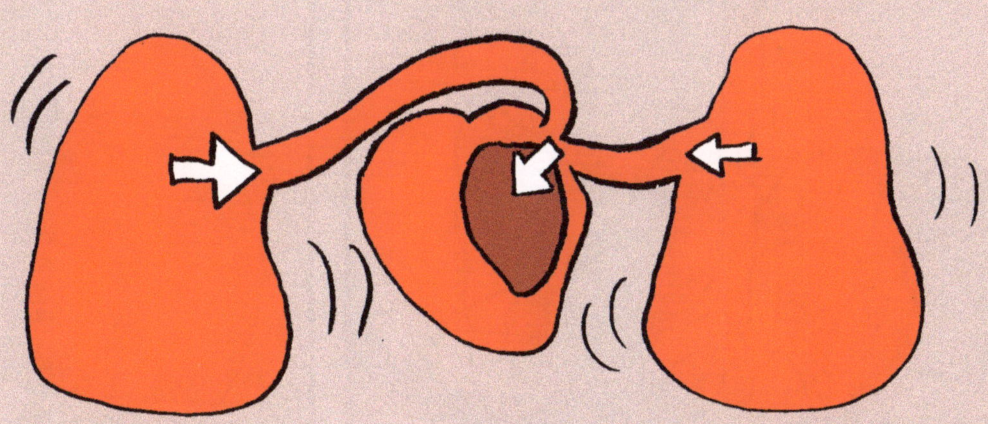

This oxygen-rich blood returns to the left side of the heart...

...and begins the journey all over again!

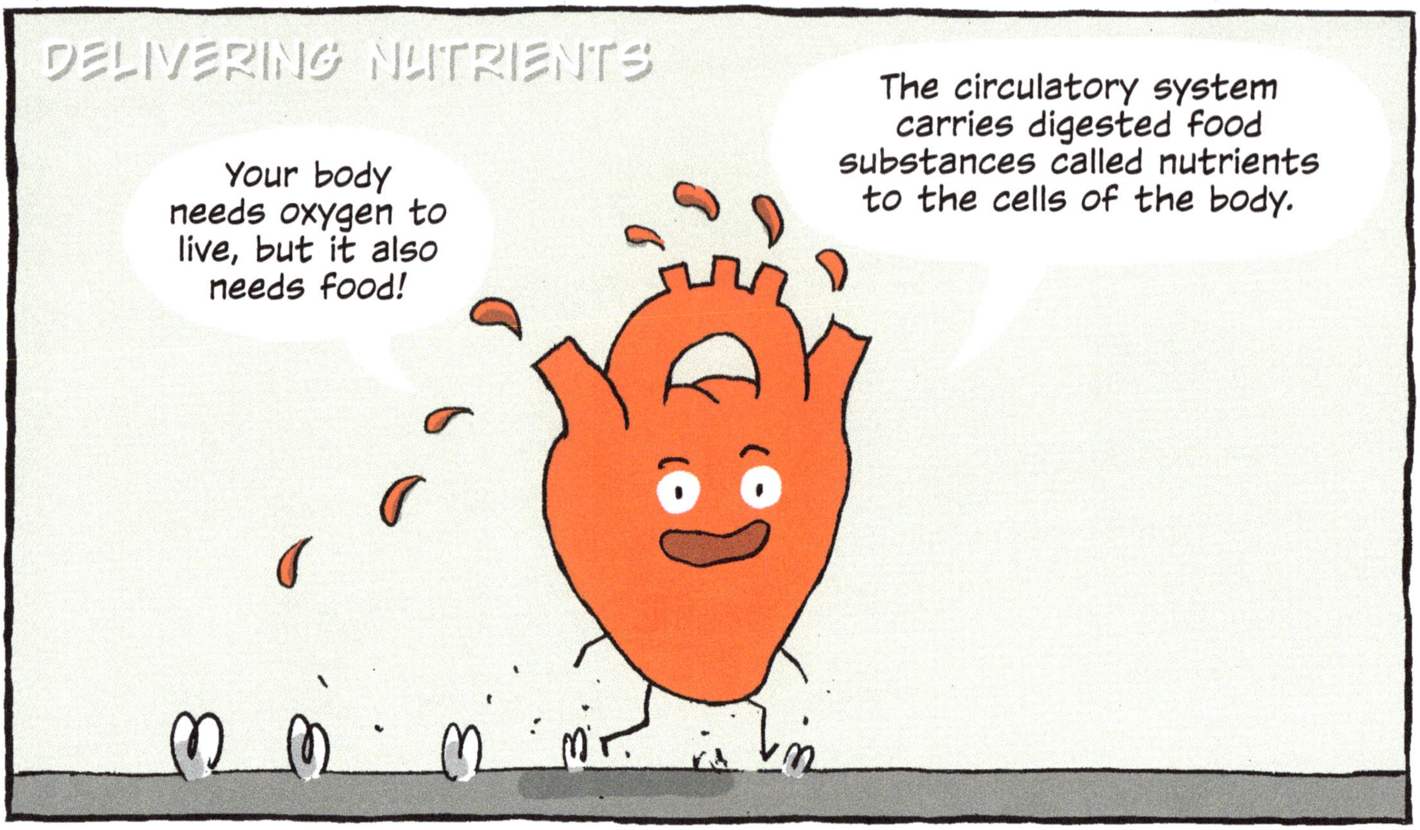

DELIVERING NUTRIENTS

Your body needs oxygen to live, but it also needs food!

The circulatory system carries digested food substances called nutrients to the cells of the body.

These nutrients enter the bloodstream by passing through the walls of the **small intestine** into the capillaries.

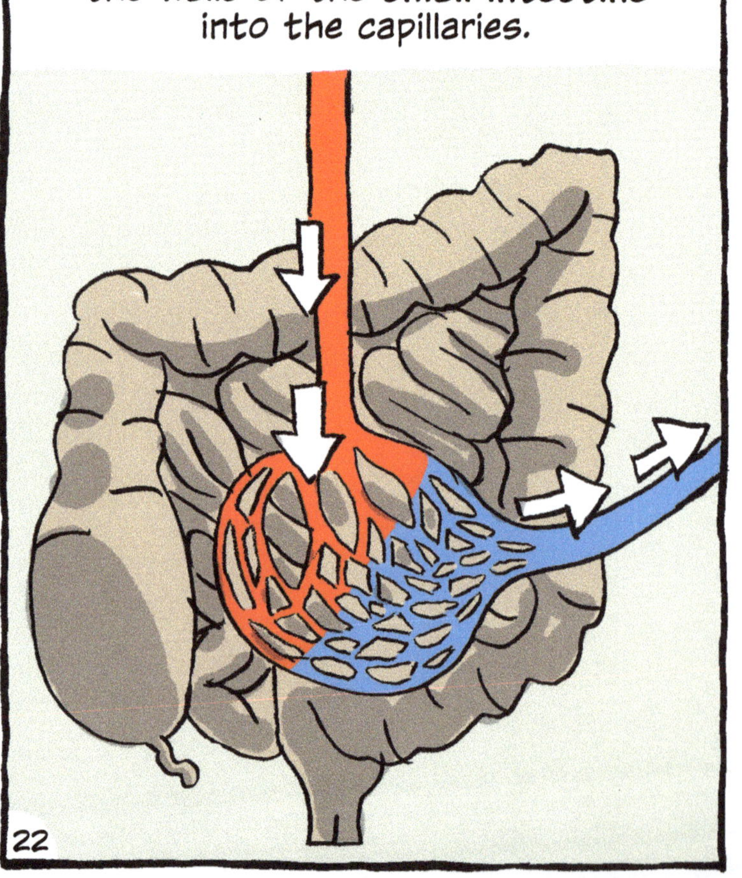

The blood then carries most of the nutrients to the **liver**.

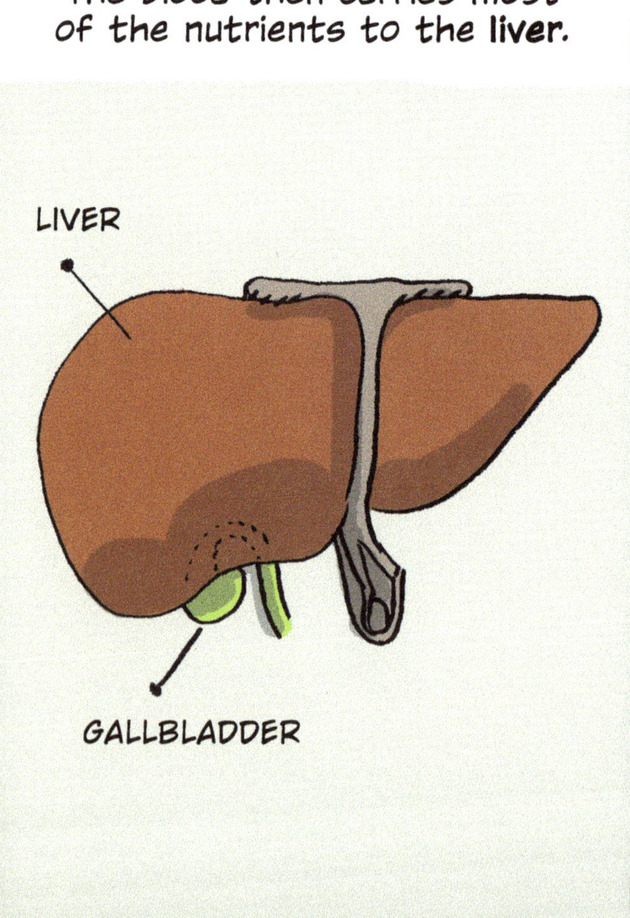

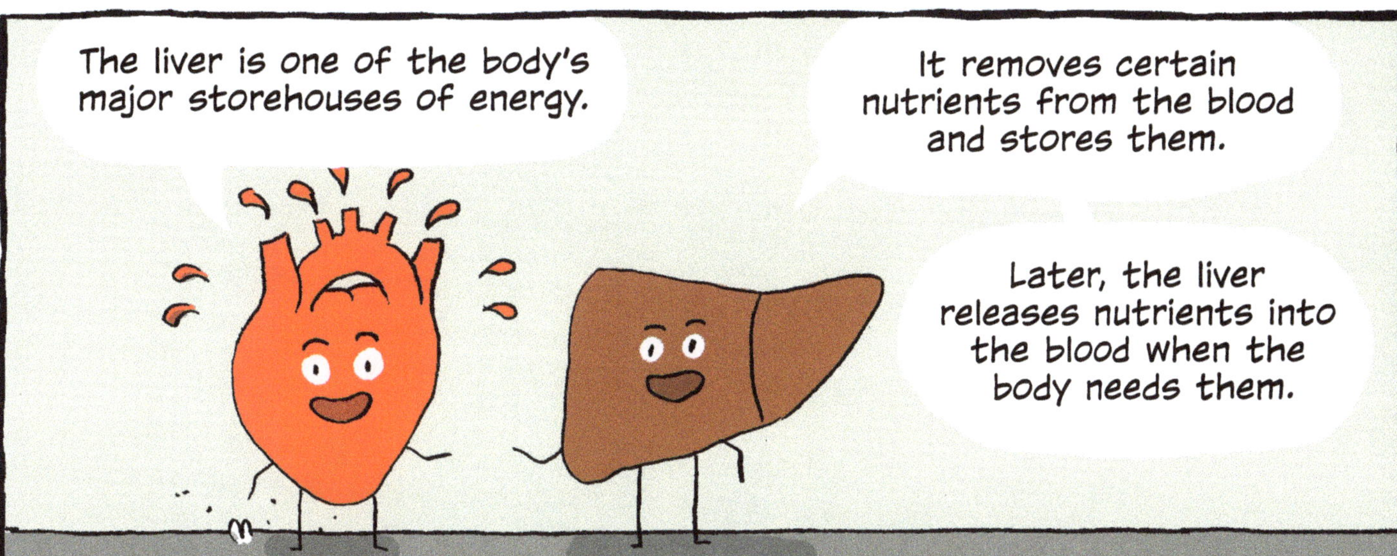
The liver is one of the body's major storehouses of energy.
It removes certain nutrients from the blood and stores them.
Later, the liver releases nutrients into the blood when the body needs them.

The liver is also like a chemical factory.

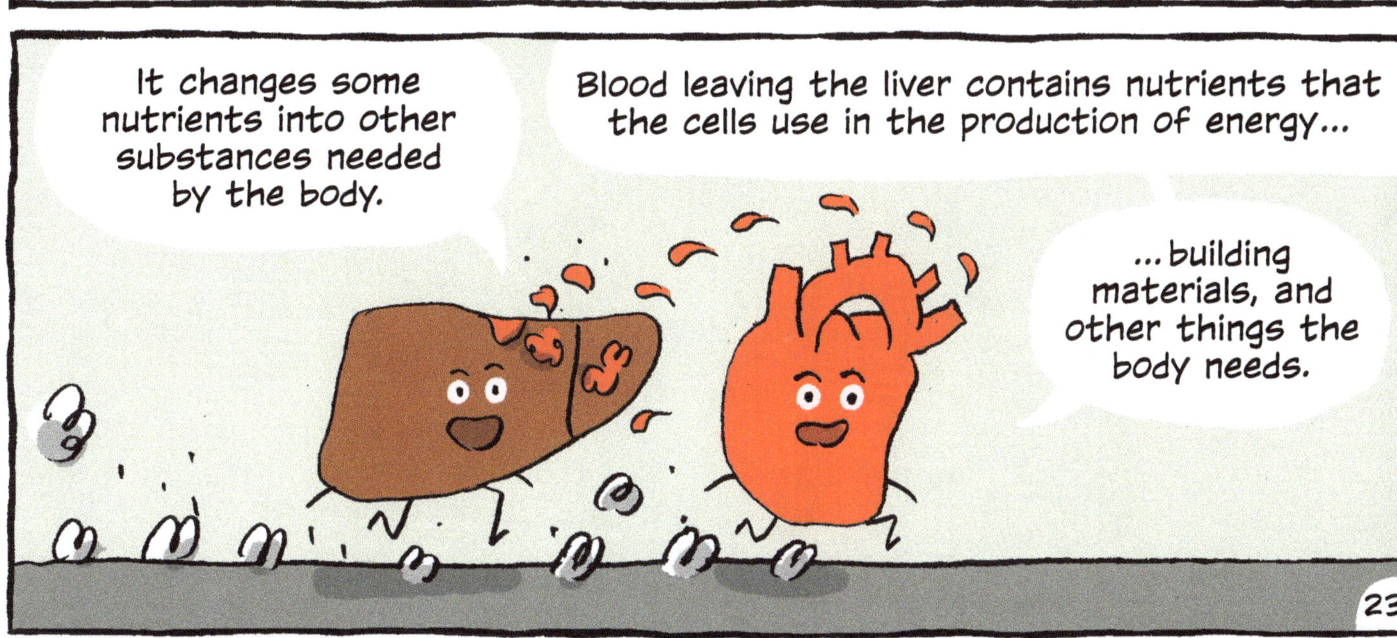
It changes some nutrients into other substances needed by the body.
Blood leaving the liver contains nutrients that the cells use in the production of energy...
...building materials, and other things the body needs.

BODY TEMPERATURE

When you perform any physical activity over a period of time...

...you get hot!

Your body heat rises.

POOF

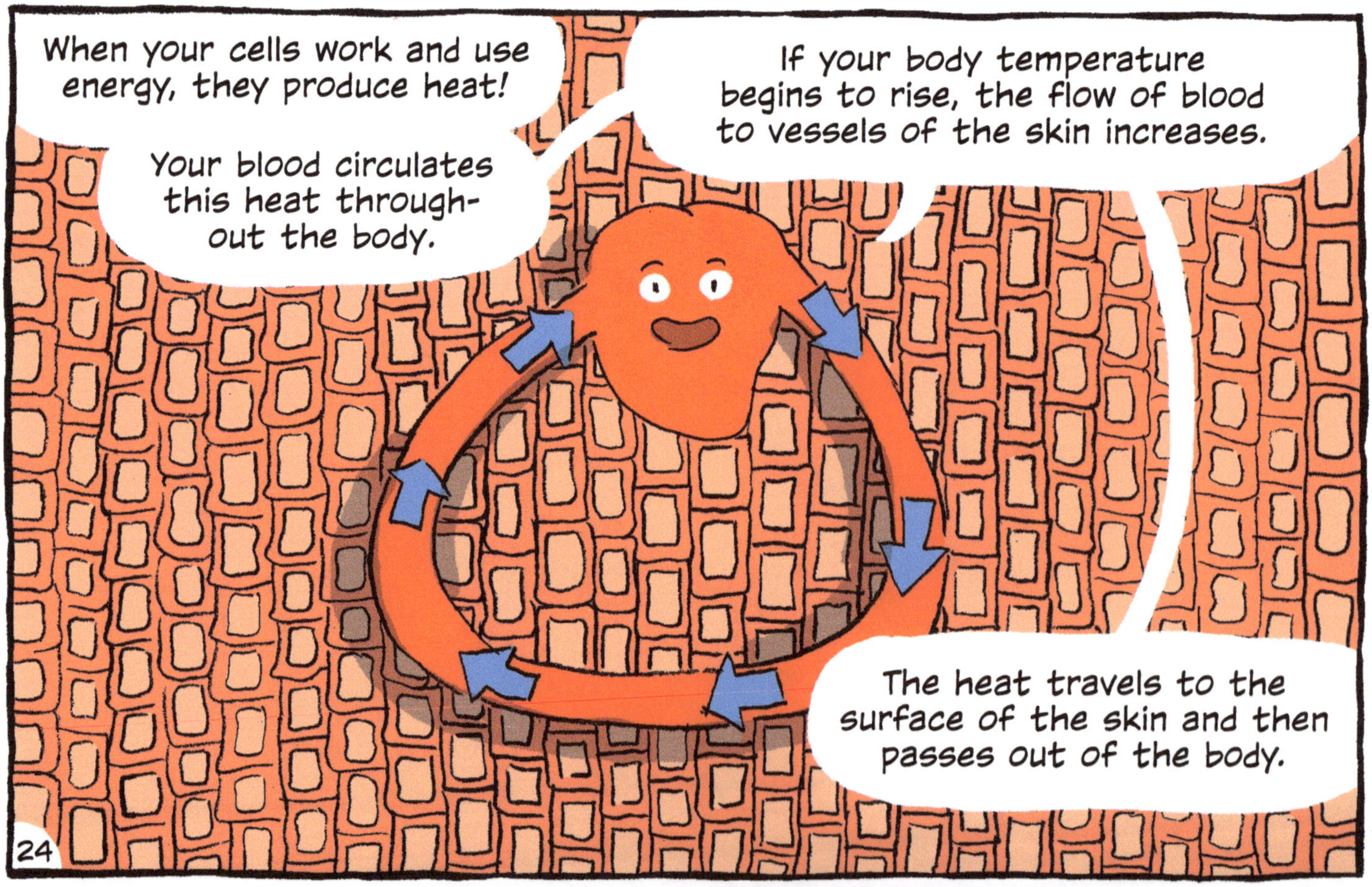

When your cells work and use energy, they produce heat!

Your blood circulates this heat through-out the body.

If your body temperature begins to rise, the flow of blood to vessels of the skin increases.

The heat travels to the surface of the skin and then passes out of the body.

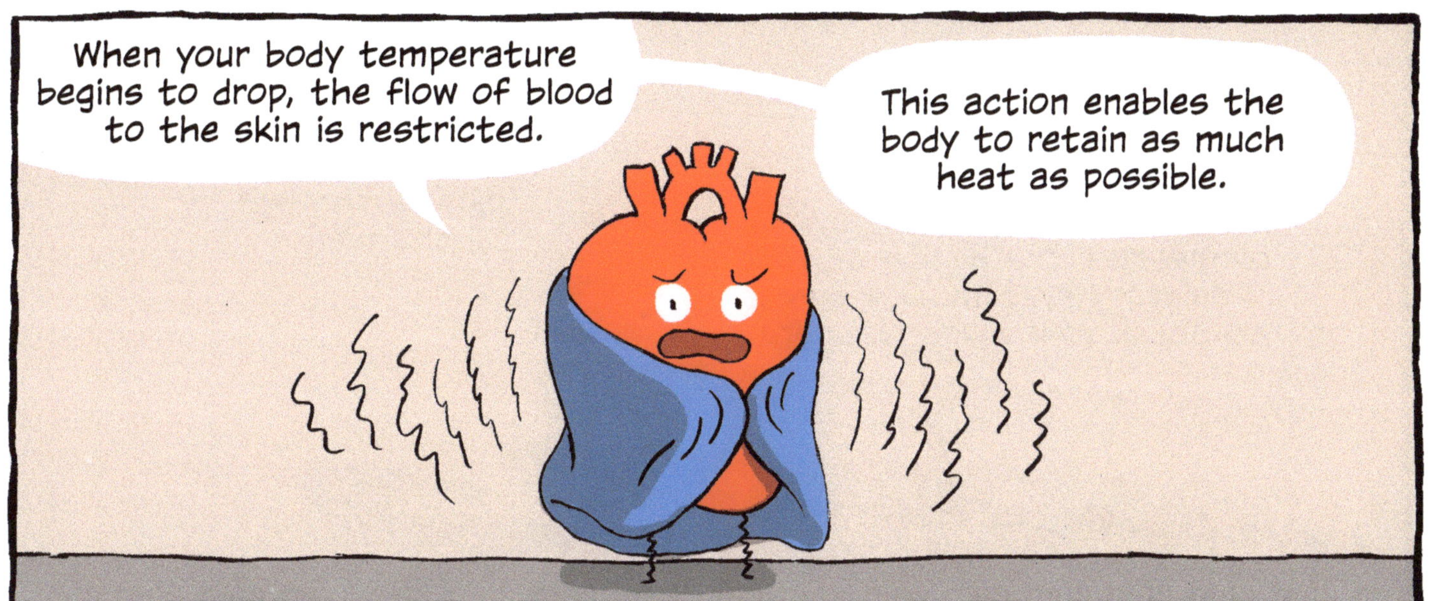
When your body temperature begins to drop, the flow of blood to the skin is restricted.
This action enables the body to retain as much heat as possible.

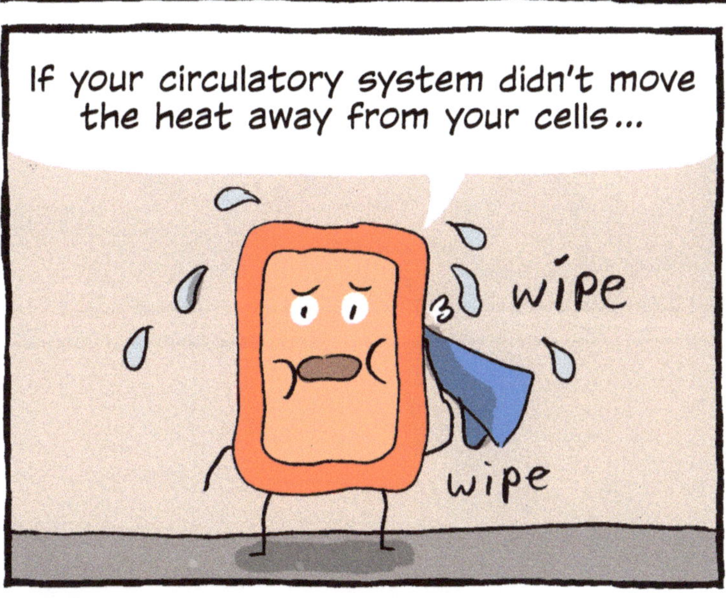
If your circulatory system didn't move the heat away from your cells...
wipe
wipe

...your cells would burn up, stop working, and eventually die!
POOF
PIFF

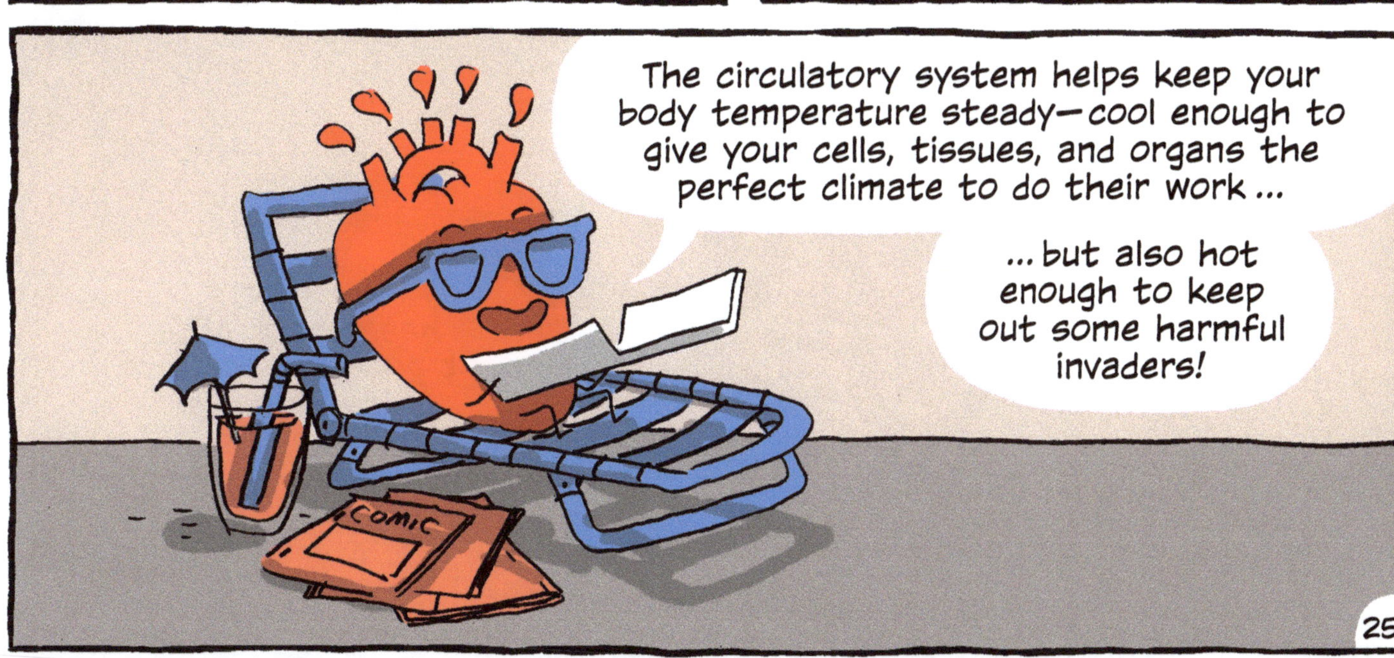
The circulatory system helps keep your body temperature steady—cool enough to give your cells, tissues, and organs the perfect climate to do their work...
...but also hot enough to keep out some harmful invaders!
COMIC

BLOOD PRESSURE

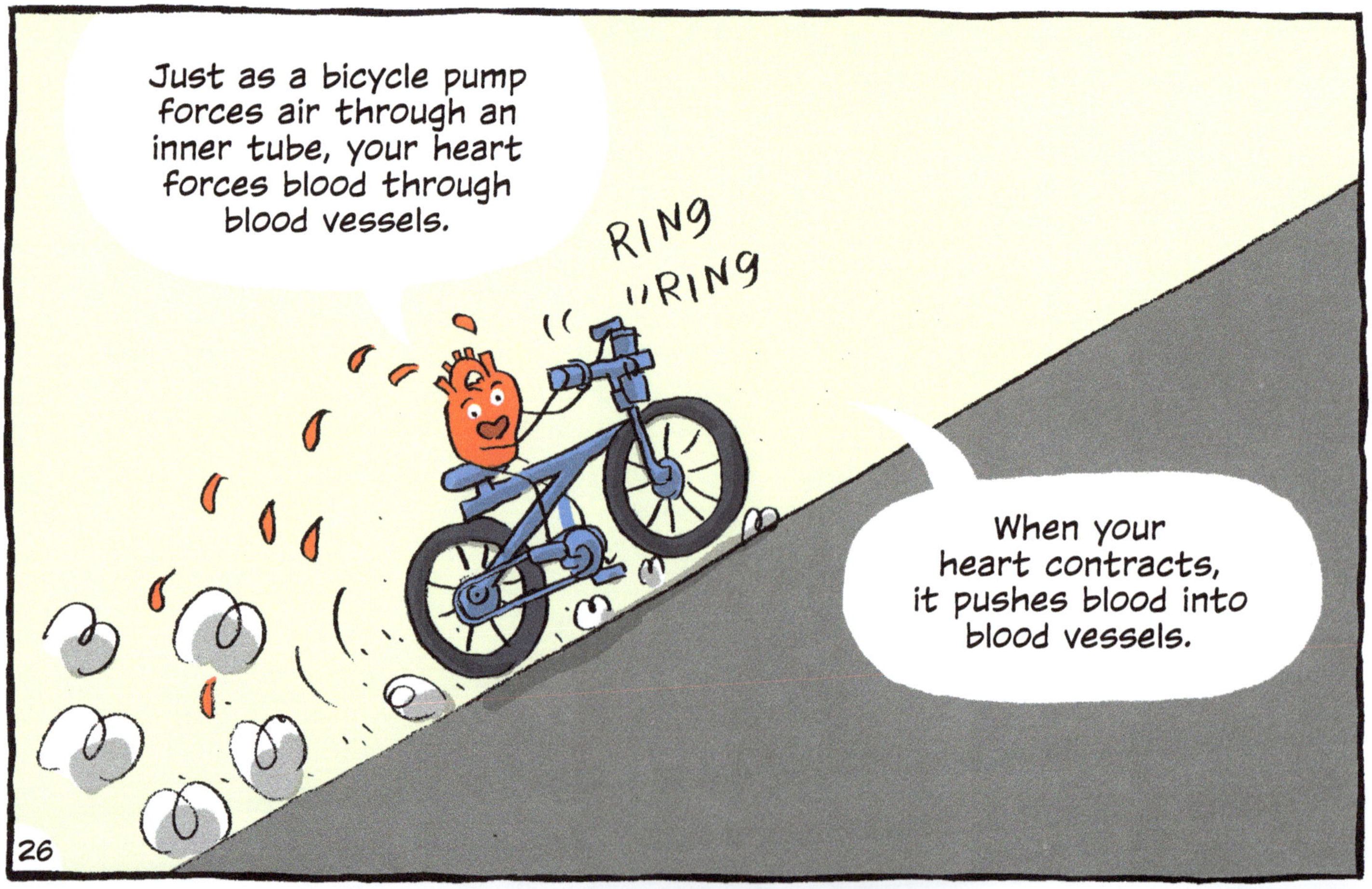

Doctors have many ways to measure the health of your circulatory system. One way is to check your blood pressure.

Blood pressure is the force of blood moving through the body.

Just as a bicycle pump forces air through an inner tube, your heart forces blood through blood vessels.

RING
RING

When your heart contracts, it pushes blood into blood vessels.

Arteries have stretchy walls that bulge when the high pressure rush of blood comes from the heart.
ZOOM
RING RING

Then, as the heart muscles relax, the blood slows down again and the pressure falls.
The artery walls also relax.

Just as too much air pressure in your bike tire can cause a blowout...
...high blood pressure can damage your arteries.
High blood pressure is called **hypertension**.
HOP
POP
POP

THE HEALTHIEST YOU
Eating a balanced diet helps to keep your heart healthy.

Vegetables, whole grains, and lean sources of protein are all good for your circulatory system!

Exercise helps your arteries stay stretchy. It also helps to keep your heart muscle strong.
This makes the heart more efficient at pumping.
HOP
ZIP

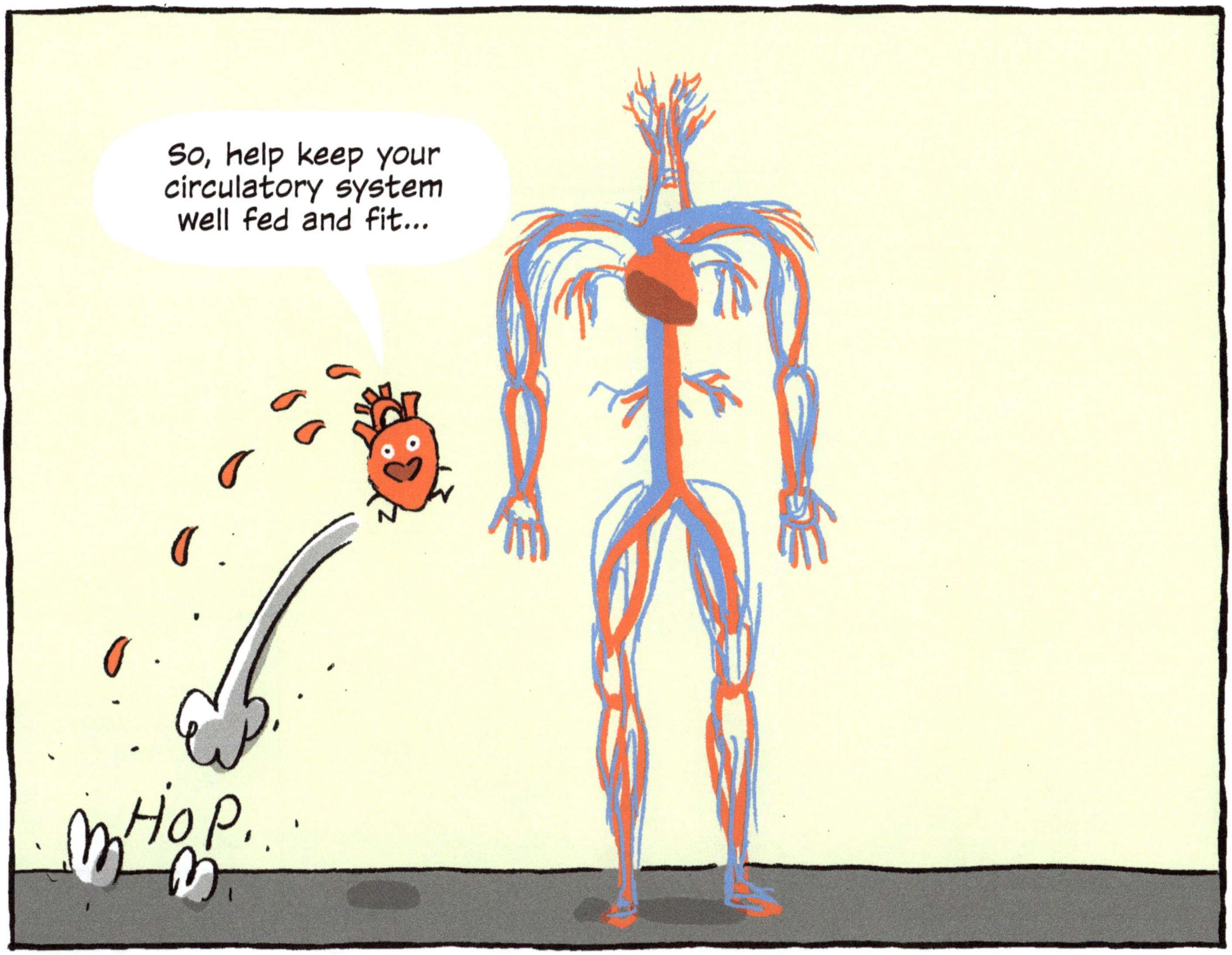

So, help keep your circulatory system well fed and fit...

HOP

...and remember, no matter what you are doing, your heart is doing it, too!

TIMELINE

460 B.C.

Ancient Greek doctors believed that illness was caused by imbalances in the four humors, the four fluid elements they believed made up the flesh of the human body.

1000

Abu al-Qasim al-Zahrawi published his medical encyclopedia. This became the most important medical textbook for over 500 years.

1543

Andreas Vesalius, a Flemish anatomist and physician, showed that the human heart has four chambers.

1674

Anton Van Leeuwenhoek recorded observations of microscopic life. He provided the first clear descriptions of bacteria.

1882

Russian biologist Elie Metchnikoff discovered phagocytosis. His work helped explain how white blood cells kill germs.

Italian biologist Giulio Bizzozero described the function of platelets and related them to blood clotting.

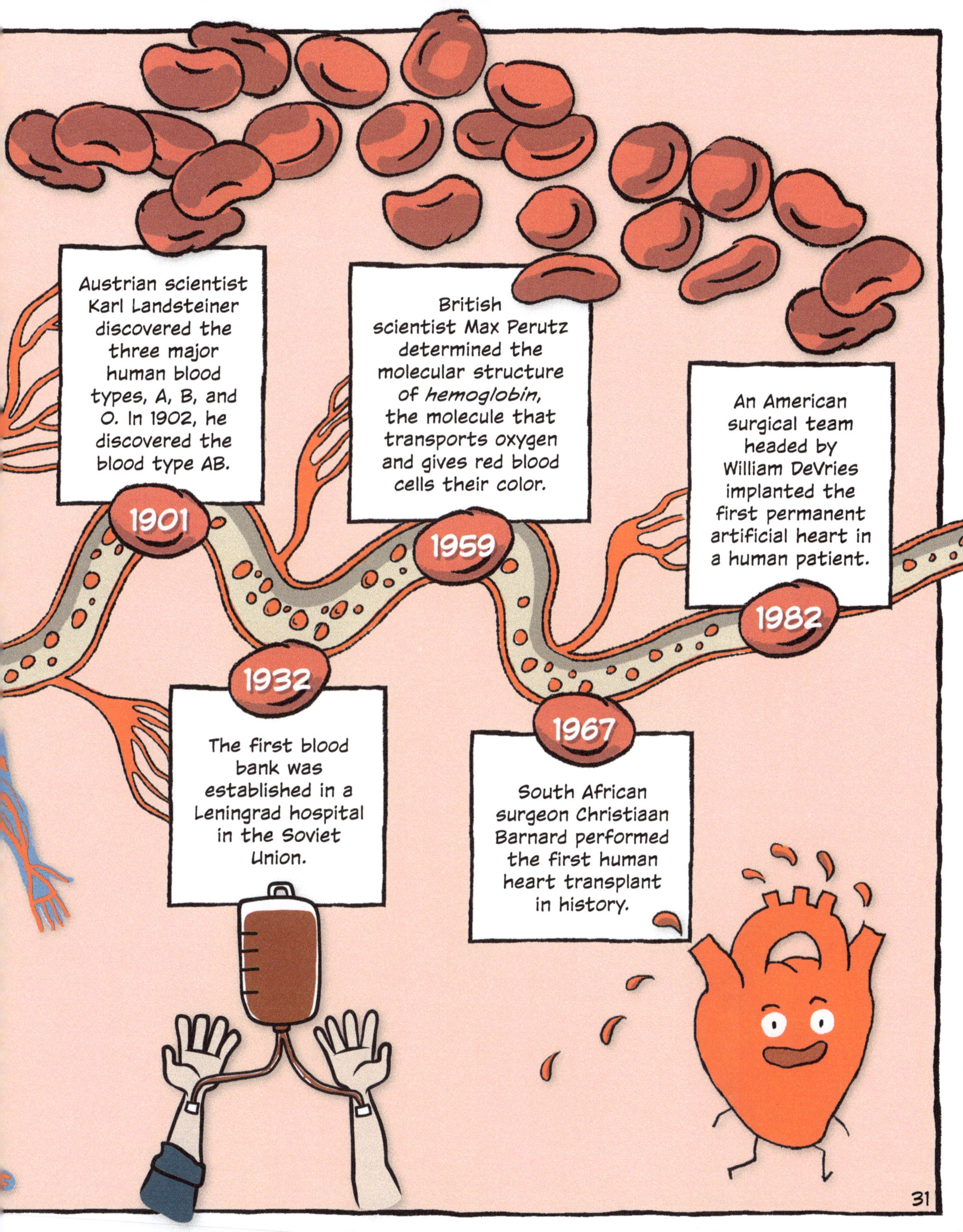
1901
Austrian scientist Karl Landsteiner discovered the three major human blood types, A, B, and O. In 1902, he discovered the blood type AB.
1932
The first blood bank was established in a Leningrad hospital in the Soviet Union.
1959
British scientist Max Perutz determined the molecular structure of *hemoglobin*, the molecule that transports oxygen and gives red blood cells their color.
1967
South African surgeon Christiaan Barnard performed the first human heart transplant in history.
1982
An American surgical team headed by William DeVries implanted the first permanent artificial heart in a human patient.

WHO'S WHO: WILLIAM HARVEY

I discovered how blood circulates in the body. I published a book in 1628 that explains it.
An Anatomical Study of the Motion of the Heart and of the Blood in Animals

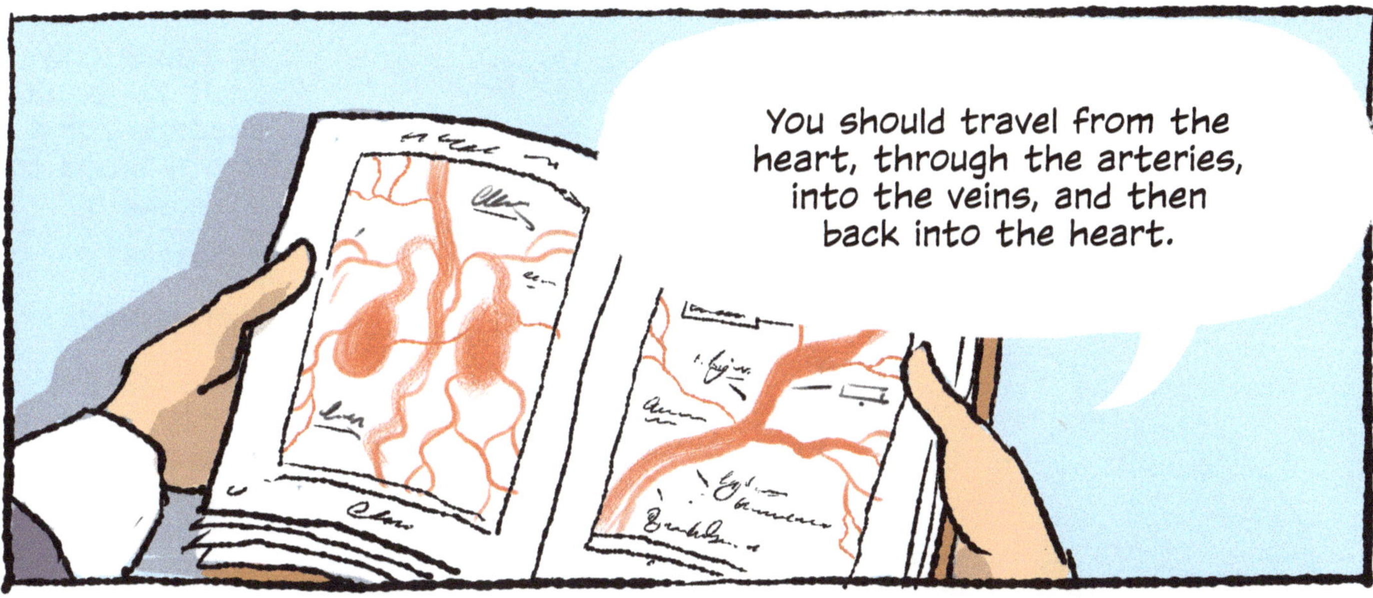
You should travel from the heart, through the arteries, into the veins, and then back into the heart.

Thanks! So, I should be going in circles after all!

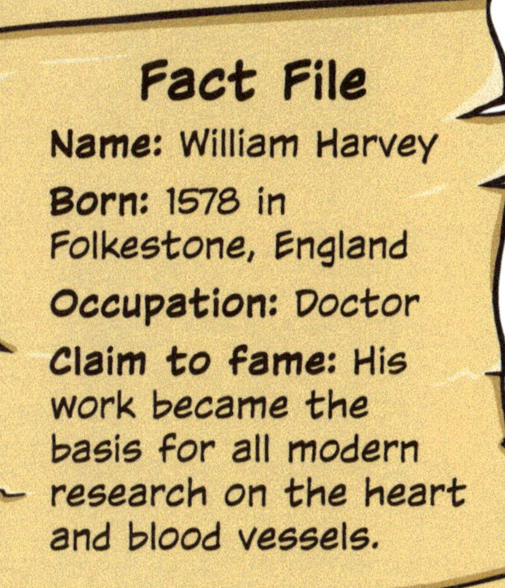
Fact File
Name: William Harvey
Born: 1578 in Folkestone, England
Occupation: Doctor
Claim to fame: His work became the basis for all modern research on the heart and blood vessels.

CAN YOU BELIEVE IT?!

An adult's heart pumps about 5 liters of blood every minute. That adds up to about **2,000 gallons (7,570 liters) pumped each day!**

Your heart beats around 100,000 times a day, every day. That works out to around **365,000,000 heartbeats in a year!**

If you put all of the blood vessels in a grown-up's body together end-to-end, they would stretch about 100,000 miles (140,000 kilometers) long!

That's long enough to circle the Earth four times!

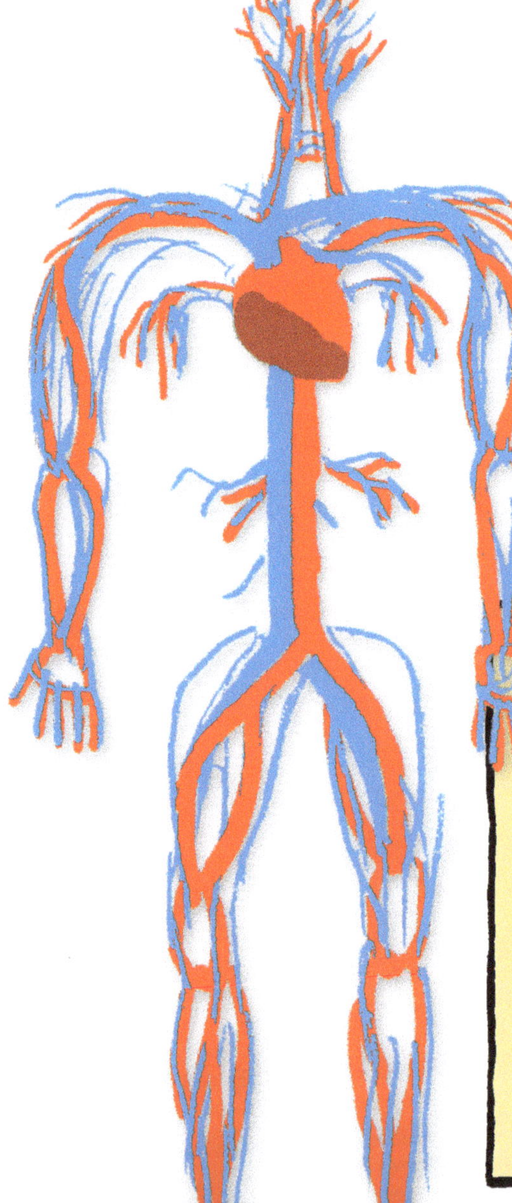

It takes only about 20 to 60 seconds for a drop of blood to make a **complete journey** through the circulatory system from the heart and back.

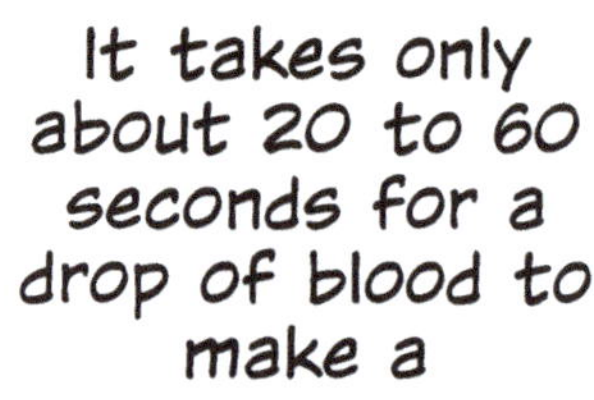

All blood isn't red.

Crabs, earthworms, and leeches have greenish to blue blood. Starfish have clear or yellowish blood.

There are four main known blood types:

A, B, AB, and O.

Type O

is the most common worldwide. About 42 percent of all people are type O.

One ounce of blood contains around

150 billion

red blood cells!

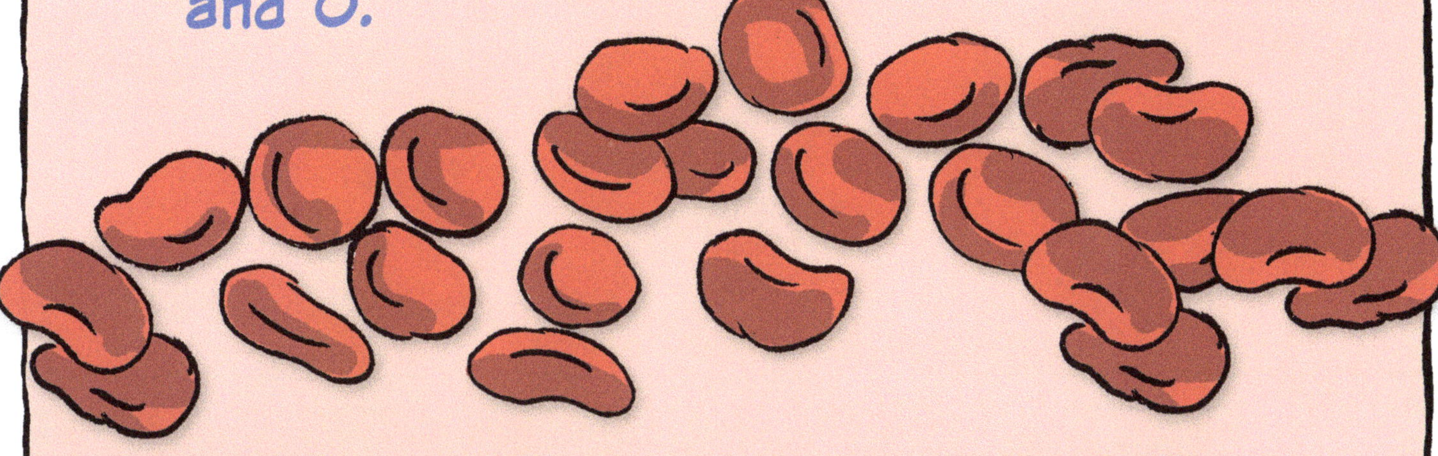

About 31 percent of all people are type A. Type B is in about 15 percent of all people.

Type AB is the rarest.

Only about 5 percent of people in the world have blood type AB.

Red blood cells

last for about 120 days

before they wear out and are removed from the bloodstream. Your body is always making new red blood cells.

A bit more than

half of liquid blood

is made up of plasma. About 90 percent of plasma is water.

ACTIVITY: PULSE-IBLY A ZOMBIE

Are you worried that your friend has become a zombie? If so, here's a way to check!

What You'll Need

- Toothpick
- Marshmallow
- Watch/timer

Your pulse is the slight thumping that can be felt at certain points in the body. This thumping is caused by the beating of the heart. Zombies don't have beating hearts.

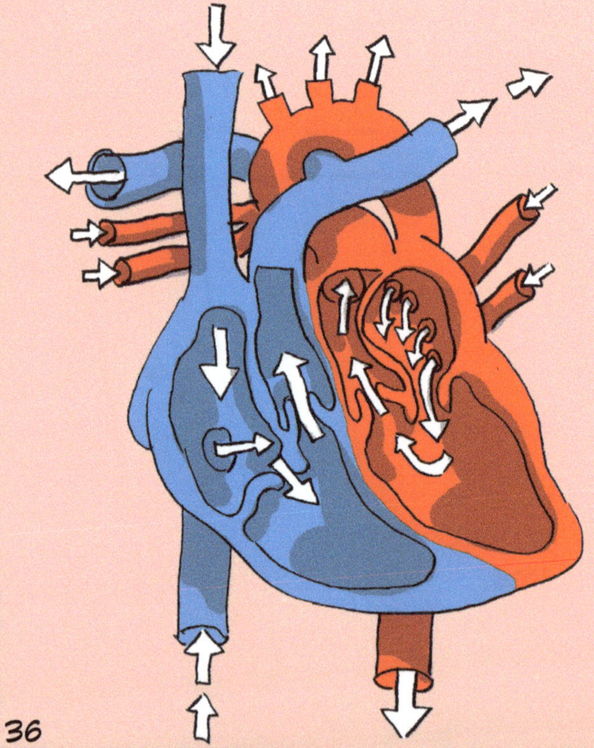

Every time your heart beats, it pushes blood into blood vessels called arteries.

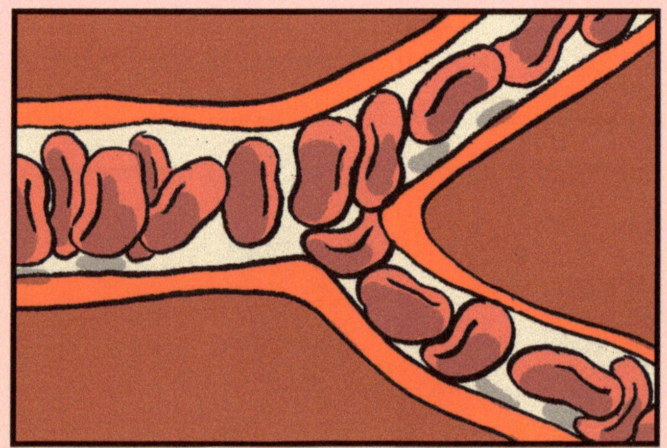

With each push, the arteries stretch a little, then relax.

Take a small marshmallow and stick a toothpick into it. Then, lay your friend's arm flat on a table and place the marshmallow so that it sits on their wrist just below the thumb with the toothpick sticking straight up.

Have your friend keep very still. You will see the toothpick vibrate each time your friend's heart beats.

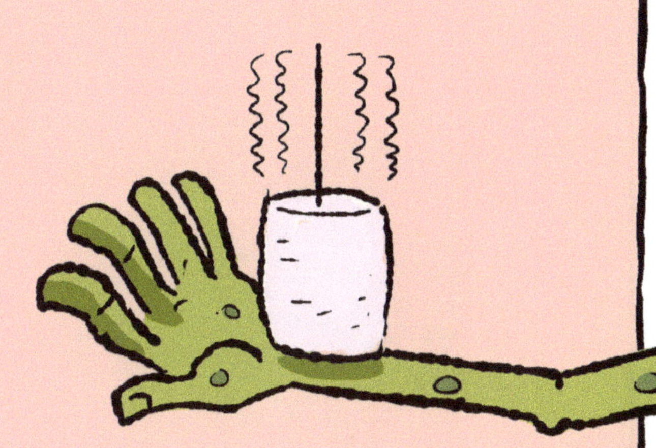

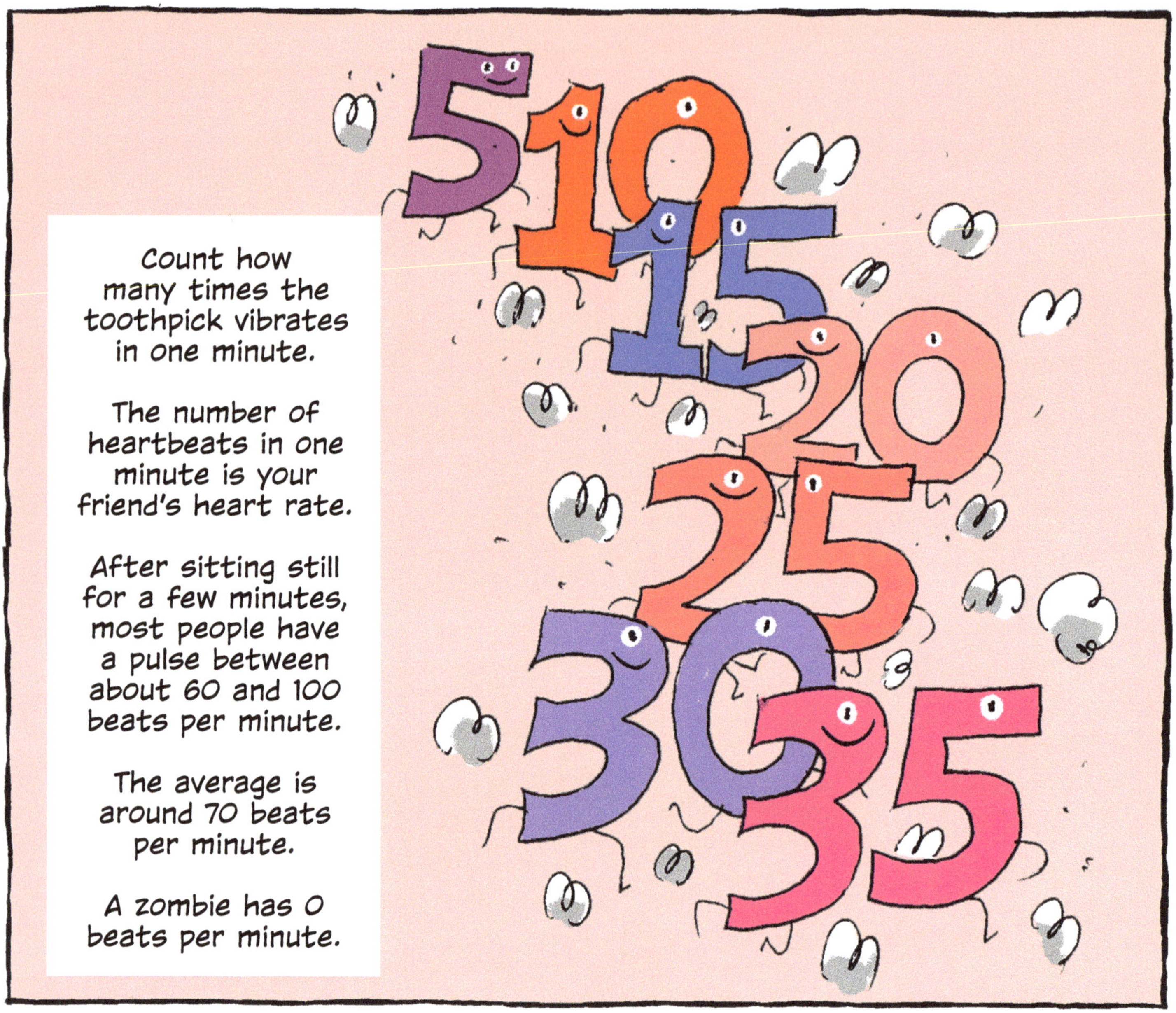

Count how many times the toothpick vibrates in one minute.

The number of heartbeats in one minute is your friend's heart rate.

After sitting still for a few minutes, most people have a pulse between about 60 and 100 beats per minute.

The average is around 70 beats per minute.

A zombie has 0 beats per minute.

WORDS TO KNOW

aorta the main artery of the body.

artery a blood vessel that carries blood from the heart to the body.

atrium one of the two top chambers of the heart.

bacterium; bacteria a tiny single-celled organism; the plural of bacterium.

blood pressure the force of blood moving through the body.

blood vessel a hollow tube that carries blood and nutrients through the body.

capillary a blood vessel with a very narrow opening.

carbon dioxide waste gas that cells produce as they work.

cell the basic unit of all living things.

chamber one of the hollow spaces in the heart.

circulatory system the group of organs that carries blood through the body.

hypertension a disease caused by high blood pressure.

liver an organ in the body that functions as a chemical factory and stores energy.

nutrient a food substance that helps body growth.

organ two or more tissues that work together to do a certain job.

oxygen an essential gas that is breathed into the lungs.

plasma a clear liquid that is part of blood.

platelet a cell that stops bleeding by sticking together with other platelets to form a clot.

red blood cell a cell that carries oxygen from the lungs to the body tissues.

small intestine an organ that breaks down and absorbs food.

tissue a group of similar cells that do a certain job.

vein a blood vessel that carries blood to the heart from the body.

ventricle one of the two bottom chambers of the heart.

virus a tiny substance that causes certain infections.

white blood cell a cell that helps protect the body from diseases.

INDEX

www.ingramcontent.com/pod-product-compliance
Lightning Source LLC
LaVergne TN
LVHW060633110826
845147LV00014B/904
9780716650669